WLADYSLAW STANISLAW REYMONT

TWAYNE'S WORLD AUTHORS SERIES

A Survey of the World's Literature

Sylvia E. Bowman, Indiana University

GENERAL EDITOR

POLAND

Ludwik Krzyzanowski, New York University

EDITOR

Wladyslaw Stanislaw Reymont

(TWAS 248)

TWAYNE'S WORLD AUTHORS SERIES (TWAS)

The purpose of TWAS is to survey the major writers —novelists, dramatists, historians, poets, philosophers, and critics—of the nations of the world. Among the national literatures covered are those of Australia, Canada, China, Eastern Europe, France, Germany, Greece, India, Italy, Japan, Latin America, the Netherlands, New Zealand, Poland, Russia, Scandinavia, Spain, and the African nations, as well as Hebrew, Yiddish, and Latin Classical literatures. This survey is complemented by Twayne's United States Authors Series and English Authors Series.

The intent of each volume in these series is to present a critical-analytical study of the works of the writer; to include biographical and historical material that may be necessary for understanding, appreciation, and critical appraisal of the writer; and to present all material in clear, concise English—but not to vitiate the scholarly content of the work by doing so.

WLADYSLAW STANISLAW
REYMONT

By JERZY R. KRZYZANOWSKI

Ohio State University

Twayne Publishers, Inc. :: New York

To El

Preface

The life and work of Wladyslaw Stanislaw Reymont, Poland's Nobel Prize winner in 1924, remains practically unknown. While some of his novels, particularly *The Peasants*, enjoy popular appeal throughout the world and appear in new editions almost every year, the body of criticism devoted to Reymont is conspicuously meager. The two full-length studies in Polish, *W. S. Reymont, Tworca i dzielo* (*W. S. Reymont, The Writer and His Work*) by Julian Krzyzanowski and *"Chlopi" Reymonta* (*Reymont's "Peasants"*) by Maria Rzeuska, are rarely available, even in major libraries. There are a few scattered articles published mostly in the 1920's, and only recently there appeared some new materials on Reymont in Polish studies. Thus, the contemporary reader whose knowledge of Polish may be limited cannot acquaint himself with Reymont and his literary achievements. The aim of this book is to fill the gap, and to provide a discussion of Reymont's major works.

I am indebted to scholars who have paved the way for my study, particularly to my father, Professor Julian Krzyzanowski, whose monograph on Reymont appeared more than thirty years ago. I should also like to express my gratitude to my friends and colleagues who helped me to obtain pertinent materials, as well as to The University of Kansas and The Ohio State University for enabling me to pursue my research. I am especially grateful to Professor Leon I. Twarog for his friendly assistance, and to Mrs. Diane Strommer for her critical suggestions and editorial help.

Above all, I should like to thank my wife for her steady encouragement, patience, and help, without which I could not have completed this book. I dedicate it to her.

J. R. K.

Columbus, Ohio

Contents

Chronology

1867   Stanislaw Wladyslaw Reymont (Rejment) born in Kobiele Wielkie, Poland, on May 7.

1884   Reymont receives a diploma as a journeyman tailor in Warsaw. The next year he sets out with a theatrical troupe as an actor.

1886   He begins work as a railroad employee.

1891   As Wladyslaw Stanislaw Reymont, he attempts to write for newspapers.

1894   A travelogue, "The Pilgrimage to Jasna Gora," becomes his first literary success. Later, Reymont travels to London and Paris.

1896   Reymont's first novel, *The Comedienne*, appears.

1898   An indemnity paid for an accident secures Reymont's financial independence.

1899   *The Promised Land* is published.

1902   The first volume of *The Peasants* (completed 1909) appears. Reymont makes his residence in Paris.

1914   During World I Reymont lives in Poland.

1919   Makes a brief visit to the United States, followed by a second in 1920.

1920   Reymont settles down on his own estate, Kolaczkowo.

1924   Wins the Nobel Prize in literature.

1925   Reymont dies in Warsaw on December 5.

CHAPTER 1

Some Historical Background

WHEN Manfred Kridl, a distinguished Polish professor of literature at Columbia University, wrote his concise history of Polish literature for American students of Slavic literatures, he intended "to present a general picture of the development of Polish literature . . . as seen against a cultural background which includes important historical and political events, the life of society, intellectual trends, education, and the arts." This seemed to be the only proper way to acquaint the readers with a literature geographically and, in many ways, culturally remote, although the method clearly contradicted "the author's theoretical attitude concerning the autonomous character of literature."[1] A similar method of presentation seems to be proper in a study dealing with Wladyslaw Stanislaw Reymont, a Polish novelist whose name, once made famous by his receipt of the Nobel prize in literature, today remains practically unknown outside Poland. Because Reymont's fiction is deeply saturated with problems pertinent to his generation and epoch, a brief discussion of the literary situation, projected against the historical and cultural background of his age, will perhaps help the reader understand Reymont and his work much better than would a purely literary analysis of his fiction.

In order to understand the spiritual roots of the generation emerging at the end of the nineteenth century, one must go back to the 1820's, when Poland, having lost her independence after more than eight hundred years of statehood, entered a period of basic changes in her political, social, and intellectual life. Divided in 1795 among three neighboring powers, Russia, Prussia, and Austria, the Polish nation was exposed to oppressions which often threatened its very existence. The first decades of

13

the nineteenth century saw that threat grow with forced Russification and Germanization, deportations, political arrests, and
radical limitations of political life. At the same time, the occupying powers prevented the country from progressing economically and sustained its underdeveloped social and economic
structure. While in Western Europe the French Revolution
resulted in far-reaching changes in practically every aspect of
life, particularly in social and economic development, Poland
remained comparatively unaffected.

The 1820's marked a significant change in the cultural life of
Poland. The intellectual ferment among the young generation
resulted in a Romantic literature with strong patriotic overtones. The patriotic movements, particularly powerful in the
territories occupied by Russia, brought about new political
persecutions, which eventually caused a reaction and a national
uprising against Russia in 1830. After the uprising was sup-
pressed, many young members of Polish revolutionary groups
fled the country and continued their ideological and political
activities in France, which became the center of "The Great
Polish Emigration." Adam Mickiewicz and Juliusz Slowacki, the
two leading Romantic poets, and Frederic Chopin were among
many other outstanding artists and intellectuals of the Polish
Romantic movement in France. They hoped to provide spiritual
leadership for the nation deprived of basic political and cultural freedoms. Poland was left in an intellectual vacuum, while
the most creative writers and artists worked abroad and thus
only indirectly influenced the cultural life of the oppressed
country. This situation could not last long. The next generation,
disillusioned, and suspicious of the Romantic ideology, gradually
began to assume national leadership; by the early 1850's the
influence of the Romantic writers had faded away.

But the goal of national political independence was still alive,
and the patriots, although deeply divided in their political
ideologies, again gathered forces in a new national uprising in
1863. Once more, however, they were defeated by the occupying
powers. The Romantic spirit had proved ineffective as a political
weapon, and the two disastrous attempts at regaining independence by force produced more misery for the nation than any

positive results. It was obvious that, since the very existence of the nation was at stake, only a radical change in ideology and political methods could secure the nation's survival.

After the failure of the uprising in 1863 a new movement, based on Positivist philosophy, called for the "organic work" of rebuilding Poland's economy, for spreading education, and healing the most acute social ills. The Positivists, mostly scientifically oriented young men and women, instead of advocating a direct opposition to the occupying powers, tried to find peaceful answers to the social and economic questions, and devoted their efforts to the improvement of general living conditions in Poland. They expressed their views in theoretical publications and also in fiction dealing with contemporary problems. Warsaw once more became the center of intellectual life, its newspapers and journals serving as a tribune for the new breed of journalists and writers engaged in heated discussions of contemporary issues, later known as "a fight between the old and the new press." From their ranks emerged, among others, famous novelists—Henryk Sienkiewicz and Boleslaw Prus—who became the main spokesmen of the new generation. The new issues required new forms of artistic expression, and Romantic poetry gave way to Realistic novel and short story as forms better suited to cope with contemporary problems. The new fiction followed closely the development of Realism in Western European literatures and, to some extent, in Russia.

Its artistic achievements notwithstanding, Realism in literature could hardly change the political and economic situation in Poland. The lack of basic freedoms resulted in backwardness and underdevelopment of Poland throughout the nineteenth century. Traditionally agricultural, Poland was by-passed by the industrial revolution which changed the character of Western Europe in the 1860's. The country was also excluded from international trade, and the Positivists' call to improve the economy simply could not be realized. In spite of some individual efforts to modernize its economy, Poland remained basically rural, and that factor retarded her development for many decades; the lack of radical reform in its social structure was felt as late as the 1930's.

Under such economical and political circumstances, there was hardly a chance for the development of Naturalistic fiction which followed Realism in the countries more economically advanced. And, indeed, the period of Naturalism in Polish fiction was very brief and resulted in just a few novels and plays mostly modeled after French literature. Instead, by the turn of the century, a new literary trend appeared in Poland and prevailed through the first decade of the twentieth century. It was a Neo-Romantic movement, known also as "Modernism," or "Young Poland." And again, among the main issues of Neo-Romantic literature there was the question of the country's political independence, and the problem of wresting some liberties from the occupying powers. This time, however, the issues were not voiced by writers alone, since by that time three strong political parties had emerged in Poland, leaving to the writers the task of presenting these issues in their novels, poetry, and drama. The Polish Social-ist Party (P. P. S.) based its program on social betterment of the toiling masses and strengthening the position of Poles in the Austro-Hungarian parliament, thus winning an important position in the Southern provinces of Poland, occupied by Austria. The more conservative National Democrats (N. D.), strongly represented in the parts occupied by Russia and Prus-sia, saw a political solution in taking advantage of the changes resulting from the Russian revolution of 1905. Meanwhile there emerged a strong peasants' party (S. L.) which would be an important political factor in any future configuration.

The writers of the Neo-Romantic movement were not only aware of these facts in political life but also became, in most cases, deeply involved in the changes. Consequently, they were to find a new literary idiom for expressing those new ideologies. Since they had ceased to believe in the Positivists' philosophy they also discarded Realism as inadequate to express those spiritual, and often mystical forces which they perceived in the people's national awareness. Instead of contemporary realis-tic novels they preferred poetry and drama, the lyrical explora-tions of an individual's ego as well as symbolic presentation of the powers hidden in the nation. There also was a strong influ-ence of Symbolism which appeared simultaneously in French poetry and in the Scandinavian theater. They were evident in Stanislaw Przybyszewski's fiction, and in Stanislaw Wyspianski's theater.

The outbreak of World War I, the defeat of the Central Powers—Germany and Austria—and the collapse of the Russian Empire in 1917 resulted, among other political changes, in Poland's regaining her independence. After a hundred and fifty years of captivity under three occupying powers, the nation faced the most difficult task of reunification and development in all fields of political, social, and economic life. Culturally unified because of a common language and intellectual milieu, aware of its glories in the past and of its fights for freedom during the partitions, the nation nonetheless had to overcome the differences which had arisen under the different conditions of occupation. Moreover, there was the task of creating a new contemporary Polish literature which could reflect the challenges facing the country, and, at the same time, develop according to its proud heritage as a vanguard of progress and spiritual leadership. There was no easy solution to those tasks since the years following World War I, as Manfred Kridl observes, were "no more uniform in literary character than any others. Old currents existed side by side with the new trends; for a longer or shorter time they intersected, at times conflicted with each other or influenced each other."[2] And yet from those years there emerged a new, contemporary Polish literature, homogeneous and harmonic, a literature which won a permanent place in the contemporary world.

Such, then, was the general political and cultural background against which Reymont's work should be reappraised. It is deeply rooted in Polish literary tradition, reflecting its various literary fashions and trends, yet it bears the unmistakable mark of his personal style. Almost every period of Polish literary history, from the late Realism of the 1890's through the short-lived Naturalism, and symbolic Neo-Romanticism, up to the new forms in fiction in the 1920's left its mark in Reymont's short stories and novels. Many of his works also reflect various political developments and deal with contemporary issues, while his historical novels revive the best traditions established by his predecessors. But some of his novels transgress the limits of a purely national literature and achieve a universal appeal. It is, perhaps, the combination of those elements of national character and universalism which makes Reymont a novelist of major importance.

CHAPTER 2

The Apprenticeship

IN 1925, the year Reymont died, his friend and biographer, Zdzislaw Debicki wrote:

Had Reymont belonged to the Anglo-Saxon race, had he been an American writer, the very features of his character which made him an example of independence and self-help, would have brought him to the top a long time ago, and his biographies would have been read at schools to encourage younger generations.[1]

Indeed, the life and career of Reymont belong to one of the most unusual chapters in the history of Polish literature. Even though his biography might be irrelevant to the importance of his literary work, it provides an important key to understanding why his once great fame today has fallen into oblivion, at least in his own country. There was no complete edition of his work available for many years, and Reymont remains obscure, as a man as well as an artist. Many facts of his life and work either are not known or have not been sufficiently explored and critically interpreted. Only the most recent publications of memoirs by his contemporaries, and a few attempts in criticism have begun to shed some light on the novelist whose name symbolized the highest achievements of Polish literature forty years ago.

Even his name, strange to the Polish tongue, is veiled in mystery. He was born into a modest, middle-class family on May 7, 1867 (April 25, according to the Old-style calendar, at that time used in the Polish territories occupied by Russia). His father, Jozef Rejment, an organist in the village of Kobiele Wielkie near Lodz in central Poland, was married to Antonina Kupczynska, and the boy, who was given the double name Stanislaw Wladyslaw, was their fifth child. Allegedly, his grandfather's family name was Balcerek, to which the foreign-sounding name "Rejment" was later added. Later, when the would-be novelist changed Rejment to Reymont, he claimed that his family was of Viking origin, an assertion flatly dismissed by his contemporary biographers as pure fantasy. Only in the 1920's did Adam Grzymala-Siedlecki, a literary critic who had devoted a great deal of his time and efforts to clarifying some facts about Reymont's life, uncover an anecdote which could prove that the novelist had been right after all. According to Siedlecki, during the Swedish-Polish war in the seventeenth century, a Swedish soldier by the name of Balthasar was captured by the Poles and sent as a laborer to the monastery in Gidle; after the war he married a local girl and made his home there. His name was quickly Polonized into Balcer, which became for his children the diminutive form, Balcerek. One of the Balcereks was supposed to have distinguished himself with a strong vocabulary—he cursed his workers by repeating "May a whole regiment of devils take you to hell." He changed the Polish word *regiment* into a regional one, *rejment*, and thus acquired a nickname which by the end of the eighteenth century became the official family surname for the former Balcereks.[2]

This lengthy anecdote has been quoted here to indicate how little is known for certain about Reymont's origin, his family, and even his own early years. The available data come mostly from the novelist's own accounts, which he gave in different versions at different times of his career. Although he somehow tailored an official version of his life to suit the image of a world-famous author in an account officially accepted after Reymont received the Nobel prize, even such an early autobiographical sketch as the one given in Reymont's private letter to Antoni Wodzinski in 1903 contains a large number of inaccuracies which were later to be corrected by his biographers.[3] Frequently the novelist embellished the accounts of his life with imaginary dramatic incidents as if seeking to create an image of a person with extraordinary experiences. In fact, he arrived in literature as a self-made man with practically no education, suffering hardships and humiliations, and working his way up with unusual perseverance and self-confidence. It was a way hardly encoun-

tered in Polish literary tradition, and Reymont apparently wanted
to create an impression that his career was very special and individual. In the accounts of his early biography he also used his
imagination freely, what prompted Siedlecki to remark: "With his
literary and human virtues, our distinguished author has also had
a genial unconcern with the difference between reality and fantasy. His letter to Wodzinski is one of his best short stories."[4] It
was left to the critics and biographers, then, to make the distinction between the facts and Reymont's own additions to his
biography, and to reconstruct his early years as faithfully as
possible. Although we still do not have his critical biography
some facts can be stated with certainty.

One of those facts is of paramount importance in understanding his future development as a novelist: he had little systematic
education. His early school record was less than impressive—
with just one exception, an "excellent" mark for Polish—and
due to the difficult financial situation his family decided he
should become a craftsman instead of pursuing an academic
career. When he was thirteen, he was sent to Warsaw, where his
older sister, married to a tailor, Mr. Jakimowicz, took care of
him as he began his apprenticeship. In 1883 Stanislaw Wladyslaw
Rejmont—as his name was spelled on a certificate written in
Russian, which can also account for the change in spelling—had
left school after completing the third grade and was entered on
the roster of the Tailors' Guild. Seven months later he was
officially given the diploma of journeyman for presenting to the
guild committee "a dress coat, very well tailored."

But the boy's life was not restricted to work. The Jakimowiczes
were confirmed theatergoers, and they often arranged amateur
performances at their home. Reymont, who was interested in
literature from his early childhood—according to one version
of his autobiography he read Romantic poetry when he was six
—became enthusiastic about the theater. He went to the new
performances as often as he could afford to, and took an active
part in the domestic projects. There he developed a lasting love
for the theater which was soon to change his life.

Although there are no documents covering that period, we
may assume that he was also connected with some self-education

circle, an activity which in Poland, kept under the rigid control of Russian secret police, was considered a serious crime. Such circles, organized among students as well as among working-men, were numerous in Warsaw. As a result of his involvement Reymont was sent home in 1884 for an enforced stay with his parents. The year he spent in the village, forcibly removed from the big city, added to his frustration which had already built up when he was taken out of school. Unhappy, ostracized by his conservative family, dreaming about another way of life for which he was not prepared, he sought escape in lonely communion with nature and by writing in secrecy.

He ran away several times. He returned to Warsaw but was forced home by the police. After a year when he was finally permitted to resettle in Warsaw, he must have already made a decision. In 1885 he again ran away with a travelling theatrical troupe, in which he served as an actor under the assumed name, "Mr. Urbanski." His new experience provided him with basic material for his literary works. The year he spent travelling in central Poland, performing in towns and villages, often starving and freezing, broadened his mind but also added disenchantment to his former frustrations. He discovered soon enough that he did not have talent as an actor, but found it hard to part with the freedom he had discovered and to return home once more. Reymont had to abandon his ambitions, and finally resolved to become a clerk. His father, who had been gravely disappointed with the young man's extravagant life, extended a helping hand. He managed to establish the young misfit as a railroad foreman, hoping to furnish him with a steady job. He underestimated the adventurous spirit of his son.

It is hard to establish when Reymont discovered he possessed some spiritistic gifts, but we know that by 1890 he had entered into a close relationship with a certain Mr. Pusch, a high school teacher from Czestochowa, to whom he later referred in one of his autobiographical sketches as *"un certain professeur de collège allemand."*[5] Pusch, active in the spiritistic circles popular by the end of the nineteenth century all over Europe, introduced Reymont as a medium to his friends, and soon master and disciple began travelling as far as Germany to participate in various spiritistic groups.

The friendship did not last very long, but by no means did Reymont's new career end with it. That short period made a lasting impression on his sensitive young mind. It affirmed his deep faith in supernatural forces—a faith he retained to his very last days—and opened for him new vistas, both intellectual and practical. It stimulated his vivid imagination to the extent that, after returning to his colorless daily routine in 1890, he kept searching for new connections which might provide him with another opportunity to travel. So intense was his desire that he finally succeeded in getting in touch with an important person in theosophic circles in Warsaw, Dr. Jozef Drzewiecki, who took Reymont to London for a meeting of the Theosophic Society, in July, 1894. The bonds of his provincial existence were broken, and his determination to leave it forever was strengthened.

The experiences of that first long trip abroad were later faithfully incorporated into the novel *Vampire,* in such details as a description of a meeting at which the famous Mme Blavatskaya presided, or the atmosphere of the street scenes, copied from his diary written not as simple notes, but as literary impressions. A Polish scholar, Tadeusz Mikulski, who published those notes some fifty years later, remarked concerning their artistic value that

A rich and comparatively full set of Reymont's manuscripts from the period of his London trip makes it possible to follow a very interesting process of the final losing of realistic details in descriptions and situations presented as, through several versions of the rough copy, they go further and further from the faithfulness of photography toward a realistic construction.[6]

Before that trip, in the years 1889-1893, another important change took place in Reymont's life. Having returned from his first short voyage to Germany, he resumed his job at the railroad and was made track supervisor of a sector between the two villages which he was to immortalize in his future novels, Krosnowa and Lipce. Making his everyday inspections of the track, the young man kept a keen eye on his surroundings. He was to discover soon that the countryside and its inhabitants could provide him with more human drama than one could find in fiction. He began to take rough notes which later turned into short stories or, as they were then called, "genre sketches."

It must have been at that time that he changed his name for the last time, spelling it as "Reymont," and reversing the order of his Christian names, thus establishing the final version, Wladyslaw Stanislaw Reymont, which was to become famous in less than a quarter of a century. That change of his name failed to change his unhappiness; his old feeling of boredom and futility is illustrated by the following entry in his diary: "July 25, 1889—back to the railroad. Curse that day!"[7] Restless and haunted by visions of a different way of life, he ran away again and joined a theatrical troupe in Czestochowa, but only to be disillusioned again and to return to the old job for the third time.

The only outlet he could find for his energy was writing, or at least in his hopes of becoming a writer. Some of his first literary attempts, more journalistic than creative, appeared in the journal *Glos* (Voice) in 1892 and 1893, signed with the pseudonym "Ksiezak," but such work could not satisfy his ambitions. Nor could it improve his reputation among his local acquaintances, who considered him either a misfit or a failure. One can find many autobiographical details from the period in a short novel, *Marzyciel* (The Dreamer), written in 1910. But, in spite of his dreary existence and boring routine he always hoped for a better future. The leading critic of his time, Ignacy Matuszewski, to whom Reymont had sent all of his stories and sketches, answered with an encouraging letter, and Reymont understood that he had to take a decisive step. In 1893 he left for Warsaw "with a capital of three rubles and fifty kopeks" in his pocket, resolved to vanquish or to vanish.

In his posthumous reminiscences Aleksander Swietochowski, Poland's foremost literary authority at the end of the nineteenth century writes:

Some thirty years ago there came to the editorial office of *Prawda* (Truth) a modest young man with the manuscript of a short story.

I read it and noticed a talent of original brilliance. When he came the next day, I told him that not only would I publish it, but I was going to encourage him most earnestly to do further work. And from the text of his story I felt an impulse to give him the following advice: "It does not matter whether you are a believer or not, join any pilgrimage going to Czestochowa and describe its mood." He obeyed, and that was how his beautiful "Pilgrimage" came into being.[8]

A vivid account of Reymont's participation in the traditional religious journey to the holy shrine in Czestochowa, "The Pilgrimage to Jasna Gora," written in May 1894, was more than a literary success. It was his first serious attempt to combine journalistic reporting with fictive artistry and it bore all the features characteristic of his maturing style. The precisions of the details of the trip and its participants blended with poetic descriptions; particularly, the passages devoted to the landscape were presented more as if seen by a painter than a writer. The young author's story became a deeply subjective, emotional experience, depicted with broad bold strokes.

The first-person narrative told an intimate story of a conversion. An alien observer at the beginning, the narrator stands apart from the crowd distinguished by his speech, clothes, manners, and interest; gradually he becomes drawn into the intense atmosphere of the pilgrimage, sharing not only the religious spirit but also the hardships and experiences of the participants. He concludes the story with the avowal: "I let myself be carried by the stream, and I feel fine."

This was Reymont's initiation into the genre which he was to master in the years to come—an epic panorama of human beings with whom he could identify and through whom he could share the feelings of the basic part of the nation, the peasants. Although he returned in the following years to his theatrical experiences, it was in "The Pilgrimage" that he discovered those elemental forces which were so brilliantly explored in *The Peasants*.

Soon after the journey to Czestochowa, he set out on his trip to England, which provided him with new materials and enhanced his intense desire to go abroad and thus escape from the dreariness of daily routine. In his diary he repeatedly expresses his disbelief that it is possible to travel freely, to see the wide world, when just a year ago he "could not believe that he would ever escape from that ugly life, the petty people, the mediocre horizons, and the even more mediocre vegetations."

After ten days in England, he arrived in Paris about which he had "heard unbelievable things since his childhood."[9] His initiation into the world was far from complete. Jan Lorentowicz, a Polish critic living in France who ciceroned Reymont in the French capital, noted later that the young man was a "person without any education whatsoever." This did not prevent Lorentowicz from offering his visitor lodging and friendly care two years later in 1896, when the promising author visited him for the second time. It was, in fact, the beginning of a long friendship, since Reymont returned to Paris almost every year. Lorentowicz was thus able to comment perceptively about Reymont's personality, his work, and some of his peculiarities, comments which he recorded not without a touch of sarcasm.[10]

After that first intoxicating journey abroad, when Reymont returned to Warsaw resolved to work hard but full of doubts about his talent, his career might have developed differently had there not been a turn of fortune which solved his most acute problem—the lack of money. Seriously injured in a railroad accident on July 13, 1900, Reymont brought suit and won an impressive compensation of 38,500 rubles. Ironically, his miseries at the railroad were ended—thanks to the railroad. Already established as a promising novelist of the new generation, he could finally fulfill his dreams and devote himself entirely to creative writing.

CHAPTER 3

The Limelights

I The Comedienne

"NOTHING succeeds like success," said Reymont in his London notes. He knew he had to exploit the opportunity afforded by a good chance after the favorable reception of his first short story. Upon his return to Warsaw, he rewrote his rough drafts, beginning with a short story about his theatrical life, "An Apprentice," which originally had been written in 1892 and had been rejected several times.

By that time the author's files contained a score of short stories, among which at least three were based on his theatrical experiences: "Franek," "Lili," and "An Apprentice." In order to understand his choice of the latter for his first full-length novel, one must consider Reymont's psychological make-up and his position in his new profession. In the sophisticated literary world of Warsaw the young author instinctively turned to his former provincial life for fictional subjects. While he felt more secure in his old environment, he also sensed that he was able to bring something new to Polish literature. Hence, he decided to expand the story of a girl's first encounter with the theater into a novel, finding the topic fresh, dramatic, and broad enough to interest the reading public. He was, of course, also thoroughly familiar with the actor's life and so felt competent to draw upon its details—the setting, the intimate motives of actors' behavior, and even their characteristic jargon. He enriched his original story of "An Apprentice" with additional plots and motives, and rearranged his materials. He quickly completed his first novel, *Komediantka* (The Comedienne), which appeared in 1896 after being serialized in the newspaper *Kurjer Codzienny* (Daily Courier) during the previous year.

The publication of Reymont's first novel generated a critical quarrel. Was *The Comedienne* a novel (*powiesc*) or a *romance* (*romans*)? In Polish studies the distinction between these two forms of fiction is as obvious as it is in English,[1] the novel being considered as the higher, more fully developed, and much more complex form than the romance.[2] Contemporary critics, however, felt that *The Comedienne* was a hybrid, unworthy of their standards for either genre. The same critic who had favorably received Reymont's first stories, Ignacy Matuszewski, objected to its lack of structure:

> *The Comedienne* is not at all a psychological romance of the type of Bourget or Stendhal, but one cannot consider it a type of philosophical and social novel such as that by Balzac or Tolstoy. Having introduced a multitude of characters, Reymont failed to group them in some perspective around one central point, and, therefore, the novel gives an impression of something miscarried, uncrystallized, almost chaotic. The nature of the subject matter, however, called for a much more perfect form. Each novel, as a work of art, is meant to give us a synthesis of a series of phenomena recreated in it; it is precisely that synthesis *The Comedienne* is lacking.[3]

The main theme of the novel, the struggle of its heroine, Janka Orlowska, against a hostile world, is in fact presented in a rather shapeless structure. Instead of a traditional plot characterizing a romance—a dramatic action usually involving two characters—Reymont follows the story of Janka as she rejects her social position and her home in order to pursue her dream of an artistic career in theater. The novel concentrates heavily on a panorama of theatrical life—its people, conflicts, and the actors' bitter struggle for survival against the most pedestrian odds and basic material needs, with Janka serving as an example of a young person deceived by the external glitter of the seemingly carefree career. The theater which for her represented "a Greek temple" proves to be a lie, although she remains blind to the most obvious facts of that reality. To emphasize that contrast Reymont introduces Janka dramatically to the strange world of illusion. Having arrived in Warsaw from a provincial railroad station—a familiar setting in many of the author's works—

she witnesses a vulgar quarrel over money among the actors. The shabbiness of the surroundings and the pitiful situation of the actors is obvious to the reader, but for Janka the theatrical world still is as enchanting as she had dreamed. When she is permitted to act she forgets all the trivia, which disappear, as it were, under the magic brightness of the limelights.

Although Janka's naïveté might seem exaggerated to the modern reader, it was fairly common in a girl of the 1890's and it adds to the novel's realism. Until she finds herself alone, deserted and cheated, pregnant by an unwanted lover, Janka lives as if in a dream, blind to the dangers and evils of life, with a recurring vision of the Grand Theater as a symbol of greatness and hope. Her dream, however, never materializes. She is too idealistic for her world and, therefore, makes one mistake after another. Even her attempted suicide, the only solution she can find in her desperate situation, proves futile to solve her problems: it provokes only an ironic comment made by her friends who could not understand her genuine enthusiasm and tragic disappointment—"a comedienne."

Judged by the standards of a psychological novel, *The Comedienne* is not convincing. It possesses, though, many virtues as a sociological study of the theatrical world. Reymont vividly portrays the social standing of the actors, their problems and difficulties, from their most mundane hardships to their theoretical discussions on art. One of the more interesting characters, Topolski, presents his own theory of "the real theater," a reference to the concepts of the well-known French director, André Antoine, and his experiment introduced in the Théâtre Libre, established in 1887. In Topolski's vision one can almost predict the ideas upon which Konstantin Stanislavsky was later to establish his famous Art Theatre in Moscow, although in Reymont's novel Topolski keeps referring to theatrical art as a "cult, institution, religion," and the like, thus submitting his anticipation of realistic forms in theater to an elevated convention of his own time.

Such associations of drama with lofty expressions, which sound rather foolish to a modern reader, reflect the idioms and spirit of Reymont's time. As late as 1902 one of the more prominent

Polish critics, Ostap Ortwin, wrote ecstatically about a single thrill felt by the audience emanating "from the altar in a shrine, or from the stage in the temple of arts."[4] The idea of a priesthood of arts, which was further developed in the first decade of the twentieth century by a group of artists and critics connected with the movement called "Young Poland," had been correctly anticipated, then, by Reymont in *The Comedienne*.

While his novel reflects an idealization of drama, in the presentation of his characters, their physical features, their manners, speech and dress, Reymont follows the realism of most of the nineteenth century novels. Such realism is particularly evident in his ability to capture the peculiarities of speech, his faithful rendition of peasant dialect, city slang, and the actors' jargon. His vivid description of the protagonists also shows attention to minute detail. This keenness of eye and ear, always the most notable characteristic of Reymont's art, was brought to a high peak later in *The Peasants*.

Raised in the tradition of Realism, which dominated Polish literature between 1863 and 1890, Reymont was also sensitive to new trends in fiction. While Naturalism in Poland was neither as influential or significant in the brief period of its existence as it was in Europe and America, it nonetheless altered the character of Polish fiction in the mid-1890's. In his introduction to a modern anthology of Polish literature, Julian Krzyzanowski comments on the literary situation at that time: "The panorama of literature in the period of Positivism[5] composes a triptych, the center of which is occupied by the critical Realism, and the wings are made by the decadent Romanticism and Naturalism."[6] Reymont's novel illustrates such a transition.

While the basic tone of *The Comedienne* is strictly Realistic, scenes such as the death of an old woman, or Janka's ordeal in the last chapters of the novel, clearly exemplify the characteristic features of Naturalism. All details are presented with scientific exactness. But Reymont, unlike Zola, was not consciously working out a literary concept here. Because he lacked a solid philosophical and theoretical background, he relied more on haphazard reading than on any sound theoretical knowledge. Most of all he relished "real life," those facts, people, and situations he could visualize and link with his own experience. The critic, Adam Grzymala-Siedlecki, declared he had "an universal curiosity," and concluded that the novelist was not much interested in literature, while life itself "made him alive and excited him."[7] No wonder the Naturalistic credo, the determination resolved to record every detail at any cost, even at the expense of style or generally accepted good taste, proved appealing to Reymont.

He repudiated Naturalism very soon, in his next novel, *The Ferments*, which is in many ways superior to *The Comedienne.* His first novel, in spite of its shortcomings in style and structure, its superficial character design notwithstanding, is a considerable achievement for a first attempt in long form of fiction. It laid solid foundations for the further development of Reymont's art. Authentic, passionate, and permeated with the author's own experiences, it made a good point of departure for the social novels he was to create, even though it was often badly written, contrived, and psychologically shallow. It affords important insight into the career of the novelist just learning his new trade, for it contains the germs of both his artistic strengths and weaknesses.

II The Ferments

The attempted suicide of Janka Orlowska which put a climactic end to her theatrical career did not satisfy the novelist. Reymont felt that he had posed too many unresolved problems to cut them off with an abrupt ending, one which perhaps was logically and artistically justified but could not end a novel which, after all, was more ambitious than an ordinary romance. He, therefore, hastened to revive his unhappy heroine in another novel published in 1897; it was symbolically titled *Fermenty* (The Ferments).

The resurrection of Janka was accomplished by a real *tour de force.* The novel opens with a conversation between several characters who serve the dual purpose of relating the story of Janka's return home to the provincial railroad station and of creating the sense of gossip which engulfs the unhappy heroine

in her new environment. As the story progresses, those characters are relegated to minor roles, and the main conflict involves
Janka, her father, who cannot forgive her the foolishness of her
escape, and a provincial self-made man, Grzesikiewicz. Although
he is her father's choice for her marriage, Grzesikiewicz does not
appeal to Janka. After having had sophisticated theatrical
friends, she finds Grzesikiewicz too rude and too provincial. A
long period of ferment—psychological and social—convinces
Janka that possibly she could find real happiness in that marriage, although neither the bride nor the author seems to be
completely satisfied with this solution of her problems at the
end of the novel.

Basically, Reymont's creative method remains unchanged in
The Ferments, although this is better constructed, more logically
executed, and richer in problems than was *The Comedienne.*
Surrounding the central characters there appear a multitude of
minor figures, often superficially drawn, always possessing some
bizarre features—they are either drunkards, or emotionally
disturbed, or social misfits—characters who add to the local
color but also belong organically to the story. Since many of
them are truly pathological, often bordering on sheer madness,
the novel develops an additional tension by constantly exposing
Janka to their presence. One suspects that the author recreated
this unbelievable gallery of weird creatures from his own
unhappy memories of the period when he felt submerged in
"ugly life, petty people, and mediocre horizons." Such a procession of human monsters creates a general nightmare mood
in the novel very well, but such characters hardly belong to
the tradition of Polish Realism, even though there is nothing
supernatural about them. One is tempted to compare Reymont's
method in *The Ferments* with Nikolai Gogol's in his fiction
permeated with uneasy, nervous tension created by the presence
of characters who stand on the threshold of madness.

Such a distortion of reality—whether based on the author's
own past or purely created by imagination—makes an association
with Russian fiction almost unavoidable. Janka's father, Mr.
Orlowski, for example, presents an almost clinical study of the
dissociated ego, thus introducing into Polish literature the image

of the "double," well-known from such stories as Gogol's *Arabesques* or Dostoevsky's *The Double*. Although Reymont's affiliation with these two Russian writers and with others who will later be discussed still awaits study,[8] there can be no doubt that Reymont owed more to his Russian predecessors than has generally been accepted. We shall return to those connections in the following chapters where they become even more apparent. For the moment, it will be sufficient to remember that he had a special ability to absorb and transform other people's ideas and even techniques by giving them his individual artistic touch.

Some of the characters who reappear in the sequel to *The Comedienne* simply function as links between *The Ferments* and its predecessor; some work as new influences in Janka's life; some perform the symbolic function of creating new ideas, the "ferments" in her mind. To the latter category belongs Glogowski, an author and playwright, who replaces Topolski of *The Comedienne* and who, like Topolski, continues to be a temptation from the past. With his sophisticated theories about art, Glogowski also becomes for Janka the symbol of a different kind of life, an embodiment of the freedom and artistic life for which she longs. Glogowski sharply contrasts with Grzesikiewicz, who is pedestrian and unromantic but sober and sincere. Representing the two worlds between which the heroine must choose, these two characters create the tense polarity of Janka's main conflict. Her final decision to marry Grzesikiewicz suggests, then, one more compromise with the laws of human existence, and when we leave her at the end of the novel, we have an uncertain hope that she might find her happiness after her tormenting period of ferments.

Among the array of characters who, according to the critic Jan Lorentowicz, are a collection of psychopaths,[9] there appear some minor figures who have perfectly normal minds: the peasants. When depicting them, Reymont apparently expressed his feelings toward them, and he used the warmest tones to depict their misery, plights, and needs. Roch, Janowa, even the old drunkard, Grzesikiewicz senior, are presented as much more normal and mentally balanced human beings than are the rest—the local gentry, petty clerks, the provincial intelligentsia—who resemble the grotesque characters of Gogol's *Dead Souls*. Reymont's characterizations became especially intense when he bitterly attempted to settle his personal accounts with the provincial "intellectuals," from whom he must have suffered in his days of literary apprenticeship.

He despised their ideas about literature and attacked what he considered to be the exaggerations of Naturalism. One of the most grotesque characters in *The Ferments* is a local *femme savante*, the novelist Stabrowska. Quoting passages from her allegedly Naturalistic novel, Reymont mocks the whole trend from which, incidentally, he was not entirely free in his own fiction. According to her artistic creed a love scene should be written "without the curtains of Romanticism, without childish shyness," but the result is more ludicrous than candid:

"Walus! Walus! Walus!" panted Jozia, with a fainting motion of her knees pushing herself toward him, and she pressed herself toward him, and she pressed her red lips into his face, dirty, covered with streams of sweat, heated. "Walus!" Her eyes were filled with a fog and getting more and more dull; a sweet, refreshing thrill penetrated her body, and a violently tickling weakness began to swell within her, wider and wider. . . .[10]

Lorentowicz, in a critical appraisal of *The Ferments*, suggests that by ridiculing the fictitious novelist, Reymont was unconsciously mocking his own method.[11] It seems probable that Reymont was well aware of the shortcomings of his previous novel, and thus in criticizing Naturalistic fiction he condemned his own method, too, for his new novel departs to a large extent from the photographic, unrestricted use of detail often employed in *The Comedienne*. By pondering the meaning of Janka's life, her place in society, and her struggle within herself, Reymont analyzes Janka more fully, both psychologically and intellectually, than he had in *The Comedienne*. His psychological analysis results in a more penetrating view of Janka and a more universal view of existence. Even if her ultimate goals prove to be relatively pedestrian—marrying a man intellectually and socially inferior to her, raising a family, and attempting to come to terms with a hostile world—they do suggest that Reymont is now searching for a reasonable solution to moral problems instead of resorting to the mechanical ending of Janka's attempted suicide in *The Comedienne*.

That the novelist has new concerns is also suggested by the broader scope of problems with which he deals and his use of symbolism. Two characters in the main plot of *The Ferments* particularly exemplify Reymont's movement away from Naturalism. Although the Witowskis, brother and sister, are another pair of psychopathic characters close to the decadent "naked souls" in Stanislaw Przybyszewski's novels who were to invade Polish literature in its new Modernist period at the turn of the century, they basically function in the novel as symbols of love, both spiritual and carnal. While the satanic Witowski represents the temptations of the body, symbolically depicted in the scene of a wild sled ride, his sister, almost superhuman in her devotion and goodness, opens for Janka new vistas of unearthly love, sacrifice and devotion. Here Reymont tries to depart from the Naturalistic vision of life as a hell of passions and biological drives, and with the introduction of the Witowskis he embarks on a higher, symbolic level of presentation. The caricature of Stabrowska and the spiritual refinement of the Witowskis testify to the beginning of a new period in Reymont's fiction, an almost complete break with the methods and limitations of Naturalism.

The richness and variety of the characterization in *The Ferments,* which mark a definite advance in Reymont's artistic ability to handle complexity, are enhanced by his shift in setting. In direct contrast to the ugliness and poverty of the city, which sets the scene in *The Comedienne,* in *The Ferments* Reymont takes Janka back to the countryside, to nature, which serves a double purpose in the novel. The landscapes and open horizons, depicted with the skill of a painter, represent natural beauty, but they also perform the symbolic function of underscoring human emotions and yearning. In the scene of Janka's first walk in the woods the beauty of nature is described in almost as masterly a fashion as Reymont later achieves in *The Peasants,* and the power of Nature to heal Janka's spiritual wounds also foreshadows the calmness she will enjoy after deciding to marry

Grzesikiewicz and to abandon her folly at last. In another scene when wild crows attack Janka, the birds represent all the tensions and terror of her mind in her growing awareness of her loneliness in the world.

Material objects, too, become charged with symbolic value in *The Ferments*. The railroad station in which Janka recovers is also a symbol of the heroine's hopeless situation after her efforts to escape it proved futile. Janka fully realizes her plight through the monotonous sequence of arrivals and departures of trains; even a simple image of a train passing at night by her window mimics her state of mind.

Such use of symbols occurs frequently in *The Ferments*. Although they are at times rather obvious, they are nevertheless impressive, and mark a significant advance in Reymont's skill from his first novel, where symbols either do not exist at all or were crudely and simplistically detached from the simple descriptions and tone of *The Comedienne*.

In its structure *The Ferments* is also much more elaborate and sophisticated. More versatile in the presentation of details worked into the main plot, each character and scene contribute to the logical development of the action. Almost each of the minor characters or episodes is woven into Janka's story, and even when they do not contribute to the development of the plot, their actions and motives are not merely digressions. Thus several subplots, which at first glance seem to exist for their own sake, serve by comparison or contrast in establishing the overall thematic pattern of the novel. The diabolic Swierkowski, who is solely concerned with money, creates intrigue by which he hopes to marry Janka and thus become rich; a frustrated pianist, Zaleska, makes Janka more aware of the futilities of an artistic career; the silly apprentice, Stas, constantly rebelling against his overprotecting mother, is used as a juxtaposition to Janka's irresolutions, and so on. When compared with *The Comedienne*, largely made up of unrelated scenes and characters, Reymont's second novel is much more ambitious structurally and more cohesive.

From the logically arranged sequence of events we can see the heroine gradually overcoming her internal "ferments" and achieving a moral victory over temptations. Janka emerges a mature woman, a woman responsible for her deeds, who is aware of the real values in life.

This is precisely the message of the novel. Through the worst experiences, frustrations, and hesitation, Janka Orlowska abandons her youthful follies and finds her modest but sound place in the world. We can even assume that in the future she will be able to find happiness. Pessimistic as it may be, the novel faithfully renders the difficult path of frustrations over which an individual has to travel in order to achieve relative peace. This mental journey is an important contribution Reymont made to the development of modern psychological fiction.

This contribution has hardly been appreciated, and in fact has often been misinterpreted, by the critics. The most recent study on Reymont, published by a Marxist critic, Lech Budrecki, attempts to limit the meaning of *The Ferments* to "the tragic role of an artist in a bourgeois society,"[12] even though neither the young apprentice, Janka, nor her companions of the theatrical troupe could be qualified as real artists. It would be more correct to consider Janka's moral dilemma as a background of the eternal conflict between the artist and society, a conflict which in various versions runs through the novel as an ever-present motif. A similar interpretation of the novel as an "accusation of the capitalist system"[13] can be dismissed equally easily, since Reymont stresses the moral dilemma of his heroine to a much greater extent than he does any social problems and he ignores the capitalistic system which governed the Polish economy at that time. Nevertheless, these two modern interpretations indicate that Reymont's novel did not fade away with its epoch as have so many contemporary works but is still capable of provoking discussion in our day. It has withstood the test of time very well indeed.

The realism of *The Ferments* does not rely solely upon its truthful presentation of social conditions and its psychological analysis of characters; it is deeply rooted in Reymont's fiction style, which much more carefully reflects linguistic distinctions and tone than did *The Comedienne*. While the technique of *The Comedienne* employed mostly dialogues, dialogues recorded

with such accuracy that today they could be considered a linguistic record of certain social groups, particularly actors, in
the next novel Reymont perfected his descriptive style, mainly
by presenting landscapes and local scenes. He also expanded
upon his earlier use of the peasant dialect by individualizing
each character's speech. To cite just one example, at the funeral
repast at the inn, an old farmer, Roch, who is mourning his
departed wife, remembers her with the same tenderness he feels
for his cow he had lost fifteen years ago and refers to her in
almost exactly the same words. It is an analogy which character-
izes him precisely. Roch, the old Grzesikiewicz, and the servant,
Janowa, begin a long gallery of characters who are extremely
vividly presented because of their specific linguistic characterization and speech habits. Each possesses a highly individual speech
pattern, with the differences marked by dialect, colloquialisms,
and peculiar turns of phrase. But although they differ from one
another, all are peasants, whose language Reymont treated in
his novels on an artistic level unsurpassed in Polish fiction.

The peasants are introduced in this novel with a special care.
Janka's problem, "the plight of a girl inwardly fermenting was
only a springboard for the study of a group," remarked Julian
Krzyzanowski in his study on Reymont.[14] The group, however,
is not presented *en masse* but consists of individual characters
and silhouettes, some sketched with just a few strokes of the
pen, some marked with only a few characteristics, but all are
presented plastically, three-dimensionally. The ability to capture the characters of the peasants individually in minute detail
while also rendering them typical of a group represents another
success of Reymont's in *The Ferments*.

The novel is not perfect, to be sure. It contains many superfluous rhetorical digressions, and its style in some parts is as careless as in *The Comedienne*, but taken as a whole, the second novel
represents an important step forward both philosophically and
technically. Furthermore, it clearly suggests the direction of
Reymont's developing art in its emphasis on human groups as
well as on individuals who form such a group, a group bound
together with multiple ties, different but uniform as a community
of people and, consequently, the whole nation.

The problem of the group, of a community made up of highly differentiated individuals, began to fascinate Reymont as a topic for a novel on a much larger scale. Before finishing *The Ferments,* he had already become involved in making plans for his next major novel, *The Promised Land,* which is almost entirely devoted to the problem of human relationships in a rising, industrial community. His interest in the peasants' life had to wait for several years until it received its perfect expression in the most mature of Reymont's novels, *The Peasants.*

III *"Lili"*

The magic spell of the theater for Reymont resulted in several other stories belonging thematically to the story of Janka Orlowska. The most ambitious of them, "Lili," was written three years before its publication in 1898, almost simultaneously with *The Comedienne.* Its first draft was titled, "A Sacrifice."[15]

More than any other, this story grew from Reymont's own experiences, from the times when he travelled with the theatrical troupe across central Poland, exposed to hunger, cold, and humiliation. Although he never became a professional actor, the observations he gathered during those years served as material for his story. "Lili" is much more rewarding a study for the exploration of the problem conflict between the artist and society than either novel about Janka Orlowska.

"Lili"'s protagonist, Leon Zakrzewski, occupies a special privileged position among his fellow actors. Coming from a well-to-do family, he joins the troupe for art's sake, and throughout the story he remains a man of independent though limited means. The financial problems of the actor, which in "Lili" often become more important than his art, do not press Leon as hard as they do the rest of the company; frequently, he is even able to help his fellow actors out of painful financial crises. By placing his protagonist in an unusual financial position, Reymont achieves a multiple goal. Leon is a detached observer who, though deeply involved emotionally with the troupe, is outside and above the common misery of the actors. Hence, he is able to maintain his point of view even in the most critical moments; he can be more

objective and more interested in the theoretical problems of
art than can those who have to earn their daily bread with it.
Furthermore, his position creates serious social and moral conflicts between him and the girl, Lili, and finally provides him
with a way out when the girl rejects him for unselfish reasons.

It is mainly the artist's conflict with society which interests
Reymont in this story, although it is projected against a well-
developed social background and a rich gallery of characters.
The pitiful pilgrimage of Leon and the director of the troupe
from one country estate to another in usually vain attempts
to sell tickets introduces characters who can be compared only
with a similar group in Gogol's *Dead Souls,* a collection of
stupid, ignorant, and selfish landowners, people who find it below
their dignity to talk to actors or who, at best, treat them as some
sort of sub-human species. The local aristocrats in a little town
where the actors rest for a while prove to be no better, and
a casual meeting with two girls from Leon's own social level
contributes to the further development of the conflict between
him and Lili, creating the awareness of their difference in the
society, thus making their eventual marriage impossible.

Never had Reymont been as sarcastic and bitter against the
petty gentry and provincial intelligentsia as in this story. Had he
not been so much involved with the plot of the love story, he
might have created a real masterpiece of social satire and produced a lasting contribution to that genre following the tradition of the Polish writer August Wilkonski, whose *Ramoty i
ramotki* (Scribbles and Scribblements) has been recently rediscovered in Poland, ranked by some critics almost as high as the
Russian satirical fiction of Saltykov-Shchedrin, Leskov, and
Gogol.

Instead, unfortunately for Reymont's reputation, he was
carried away by a rather sentimental story and focused on the
moral dilemma of Lili. Her love for Leon had been hampered by
her embittered mother, a former actress who knew only too well
the dangers of an uneven match between a girl from the theater
and a socially secure man. And so Lili, acting on her mother's
advice, makes a fateful decision: pretending that she loves someone else, she uses all her theatrical talent to discourage Leon

from their marriage. She also has a more noble purpose: she wants to spare Leon from the hardships of a theatrical career. But to her dismay she discovers that Leon takes her performance at face value and leaves in a brutal outburst of anger which discloses his petty character not worthy of her sacrifice. Thus Lili becomes a real heroine in her humble sacrifice, giving away her love and her dream of happiness to save Leon from the consequences of their liaison, and emerges a moral victor.

The theme of moral victory must have preoccupied Reymont for a long time. "Lili," although crudely and sentimentally written, develops this theme much more dramatically than does *The Ferments*, but the dilemmas which Lili and Janka face and their ultimate moral victories create a similar thematic concern which their stories by no means exhausted for Reymont. It recurs in his later works, works written long after he had abandoned theatrical subjects.

IV   *"Franek"*

The theatrical group series in Reymont's fiction includes one more short story, "Franek." Chronologically, it precedes "Lili" and the two novels related to the theater by about three years, and together with "The Apprentice"—the first version of *The Comedienne*—it belongs to Reymont's early attempts at prose in 1892. It is, however, a more serious story than one might expect from a beginner, for in the characterization of Franek it poses the problem of an artistic ambition in an individual who is rejected by society on the grounds of mental and social unfitness.

Characters like Franek have a long tradition in Polish literature. Two leading Realistic novelists, Boleslaw Prus and Henryk Sienkiewicz, had written moving stories in which they appeal for the recognition of natural talents in those deprived of an education or, simply, of luck. Sienkiewicz in his "Yanko the Musician" (1879) created a moving drama of a child who dreams of playing a real violin and meets with severe punishment and eventual death. Prus's story "Antek" poses a similar problem and offers no suggestions for the alleviation of such individual tragedies except public understanding and charity. Reymont moves

an almost identical problem into the theater. Instead of repeating his predecessors' subjects—children deprived of a chance
in life—he fashioned his story in a naturalistic manner by focus-
ing on an imbecile, Franek, who is, obviously, totally devoid of
talent. Instead, Reymont equips him with a real passion for the
theater, a passion which finds eventual expression in an ambition
to write, an ambition stronger than any humiliation, scorn, or
hardship Franek has to meet. Working as a drudge in a theater
he is suddenly obsessed with the idea of becoming a playwright,
with actively securing his place in that world of which he had
always dreamed. Night after night he works on a theatrical
adaptation of a popular novel, *Ulana*, by the Polish novelist
Jozef Ignacy Kraszewski, and despite a complete lack of talent
or education, he finally succeeds in writing four acts of the play.

In a sudden turn of events Franek loses the manuscript. He
manages to overcome his grief and starts all over again, determined to complete his work. "He was resolved to win," Reymont concludes the story, adding an unfounded optimistic note
to Franek's boast that the public would howl with joy after
seeing the play performed: "Maybe they will. Who knows?"

"Franek" does not rank among Reymont's masterpieces. His
story develops amid scenes of wild, mad, distasteful orgies, and
on the whole is full of meaningless dialogues overloaded with
theatrical jargon. It is preoccupied with sex and abnormal
characters. If we apply the definition proposed by Donald W.
Heiney that "the real motivating forces in a Naturalistic novel
are not religion, hope, or human idealism, they are alcohol,
filth, disease, and the human instinct toward bestiality,"[16] we
may consider "Franek" a significant stage in Reymont's artistic
development, for it is this Naturalistic environment precisely
which he depicts in this story. The conflict between a protagonist
and his environment, another characteristic of Naturalism,
became one of the central concerns in Reymont's fiction in the
first stage of his literary career, as in *The Comedienne* and some
of his short stories written in the 1890's. In general, however,
we may safely assume that after "Franek" he overcame the main
impact of Naturalism on his art, and began to reject and ridicule
its methods as in *The Ferments*. He retained some of its motifs

and devices, but Reymont never followed the paths of Zola or Gorky, who could not see any hope for human beings entangled in the brutal and cruel materialistic environment of their lives. His faith in the human race was stronger than any of the literary influences he eagerly accepted, but transformed into his own vision. For no matter how depressing life may have been, Reymont never abandoned hope for the human spirit.

It took him, however, a long time to return to the unfounded, optimistic conclusion he had reached in "Franek" and to affirm this hope in the human experience. He had to go through Dantesque scenes in his earlier short stories of the peasants' lives, through the misery of theatrical existence, and through the modern jungle of an industrial metropolis before he could discern and reveal the eternal order of things in his epic novel, *The Peasants*.

The novels and stories devoted to life in the theater were but a first step in that long journey.

CHAPTER 4

In the Polish Manchester

I   The City of Lodz

BEFORE *The Ferments* was completed in September 1896, Reymont wrote to Lorentowicz about a new novel, which was already absorbing him:

For me Lodz is a mystical economic power, it does not matter whether wrong or good, but it is a power which embraces with its domination ever wider and wider human circles, which devours the peasant, tears him from the soil and uproots him; and it does the same to an intellectual, the same to a jobber taken at random, the same to the worst one, and to a worker—it is a huge stomach digesting people and land, only a stomach, always hungry.[1]

It is no wonder that the city of Lodz captured Reymont's imagination. From a small village, it had expanded into an industrial city in a few years when the rapid growth of manufacturing in the second half of the nineteenth century had brought in hundreds of thousands of workers. In 1860 there were 32,000 residents; by 1900 their number exceeded 310,000. Along with industry and the population grew "the city, the fortunes, and the business with a real American speed," as Reymont said to Lorentowicz.

For a novelist as sensitive to the problems of community and of human groups as was Reymont, Lodz presented a psychosociological, and, consequently, artistic challenge. He was less concerned with the economic problems of trade or the technology of industry than were some of his predecessors or contemporaries, nor did he primarily care about the effects of making money on an individual, the theme of a major Polish novel, *The Doll* (1890), by Reymont's contemporary, Boleslaw

44

Prus. Reymont wanted rather to explore the "melting pot" of
Lodz and the three ethnic groups which made it grow: Poles,
Jews, and Germans, for it was just the combination of Polish
labor, Jewish capital, and German technology which contributed
to the expansion of the "Polish Manchester," a manufacturing
giant of its time.

Reymont himself had not lived in Lodz, but he was born in
the immediate vicinity and spent many years there. He must have
had friends and relatives who had been affected by the rapid
growth of the industrial metropolis in the middle of a rural
area. An artistic stimulus to writing about Lodz was at hand,
too. In 1895, just before Reymont began writing, the novel
Bawelna (Cotton) by Wincenty Kosiakiewicz, achieved wide
popularity as the first Polish novel concerned with industrialization, and in particular with Lodz. Apparently having exhausted
the theatrical theme in his first two novels and early short
stories, Reymont confronted the industrial city, fascinated by the
multitude of possibilities suggested by its social and psychological complexity. The instinct of a novelist must have told
him that the topic would prove fruitful, and *Ziemia obiecana*
(The Promised Land), the resulting novel, has few equals in
literature even now. In its ambitious scope it can stand comparison with Dos Passos's *Manhattan Transfer* or Valentin
Kataev's *Time, Forward!*, both written a quarter of a century
after Reymont's pioneering work.

The city of Lodz provided a spectacular setting. Industry was
changing a provincial town into a modern metropolis, creating
striking contrasts and violent conflicts. Huge factories sprang
up in the middle of fields; luxurious restaurants and theaters
grew along with shabby apartment houses; crowds dressed in the
latest fashion mingled with Orthodox Jews and peasants in
colorful costumes; all were enveloped by the enormous clouds
of smoke spouting from thousands of chimneys, smoke which
threw dirty shadows on everything in this city of tensions.

Reymont centered his interest on the Polish, German, and
Jewish inhabitants of the city. Different in their ways of life,
education, experience, and even language, the Poles, Germans,
and Jews came together only in the common pursuit of business

and created contrasts seldom encountered before in Poland or the rest of Europe. Although Reymont naturally enough focused first on his Polish compatriots, as the novel develops, he balances his presentation of the three groups.

The Poles in *The Promised Land* are primarily of three basic groups: the technical intelligentsia, most of whom originated in the landed gentry, the impoverished landowners who had lived near Lodz, and the workers who are of peasant stock. The latter group, incidentally, receives the least attention in the novel, as if Reymont could not force himself to depict their decline in the city slums. Less stratified are the Germans, who are, in the main, industrial tycoons or skilled technicians, deeply devoted to their workshops and factories. Even more heterogeneous are the Jewish businessmen, entirely devoted to making a profit in more or less tricky ways.

To deal with a multitude of problems among the three groups, Reymont uses a device foreign to the standard Realistic novel and expands the traditional limitation of fiction to individual characters by encompassing national groups. He wrote a "novel without a hero" by concentrating almost equally upon three characters, each representative of his nationality: Karol Borowiecki, a Polish engineer; Max Baum, a German technician, and Moryc Welt, a Jewish businessman. Borowiecki emerges as the strongest character and becomes by the end the protagonist, but initially that role is shared by all three. Throughout, Reymont works to present each character's virtues and vices objectively.

Although he is intelligent and energetic, the Pole, Borowiecki, then, is by no means a character of uniformly heroic proportions; he is often reckless, particularly with women. Moryc Welt, the least sympathetically drawn of the three, cheats his associates and dwells on financial matters most of the time. Max Baum, a devoted friend and a highly skilled technician, is sentimental and often passive at decisive moments. Each is shown in his best and worst lights and in his relationship with the others. As the novel opens, the three friends are starting an industrial enterprise, hoping that each will contribute his best. Their potential factory soon recedes into the background, however, as Reymont emphasizes the entire industrial jungle. He begins to shift characters and scenery, starts and drops new plots, flashes vignettes and scenes with staggering speed, using as it were, a movie technique in fiction. The novelist proves to be a diligent director of his imaginary film; there is order in the kaleidoscopic presentation of Lodz, and he never loses control over his characters and their fates. Sub-plots, crossing and interweaving with one another, move the action forward, and the panorama of the city comes to life as the action progresses.

Borowiecki's affair with his mistress, Lucy, helps him to get important information about the new tariffs on imported cotton and sets in motion the activities of Welt, who eventually discloses his real nature while trying to deceive his partners. Later, Borowiecki's and Baum's trip to see Borowiecki's fiancée seemingly only introduces a break in the tense tempo of business and industrial transactions, but it also reveals Borowiecki's real character to Baum and changes his attitude toward Borowiecki, who does not deserve to be trusted. Simultaneously, the trip introduces several new characters and problems which eventually further develop the main plot. The accumulation of characters, who are differentiated so much that Lorentowicz did not hesitate to label them "a noisy gang made up of eighty-two individuals,"[2] all fuse into a peculiar unity; this new method of making a novel with hundreds of them in a highly unified crowd plays an important role in the new novelistic technique introduced by Reymont.

Reymont did not intend to write a Polish epic version of *War and Peace* or the Rougon-Macquart cycle by Zola. Limiting himself to Lodz and its problems he manipulates characters and scenes, introducing and removing them often to emphasize the social and psychological make-up of a rising industrial city. Reymont's characters perform a vital function in conveying the sense of the city, but they do not have a universal meaning. By its very nature, the novel focuses not on family relationships, but rather on uprooted characters coping with a new environment. Thus Reymont departed from the European traditions of Realism and Naturalism, which attempted an all-embracing epic presentation, and fashioned family sagas that explored the interrelationships and conflicts among a group of kinsmen. In this respect *The Promised Land* is much closer to American naturalistic novels such as Dreiser's and Crane's than to Reymont's European predecessors.

II   *The Law of the Jungle*

Reymont surrounded the three main characters of the novel with a diversified crowd united by one common feature. He labeled them all as the *"Lodzer-Mensch,"* a German term denoting people with a ruthless drive for riches. This, he felt, was the common denominator of the people who made Lodz unique and, therefore, worth a thorough exploration in fiction. Naturally then, he devotes a substantial part of *The Promised Land* to financial tycoons and their business, and his juxtaposing them with those who could not succeed because they could not withstand the competition underscores that point. While Borowiecki and his factory represent the new methods in business and industry, methods superficially more honest than those used by the big businessmen of the previous generation, a close examination of the protagonist's records proves that he is not devoid of cunning and fraud of *"Lodzer-Mensch."* However, the representatives of big business, particularly the Germans and Jews, best exemplify *"Lodzer-Menschen."* Some are drawn with irony, like Müller, an unsophisticated millionaire who has an appetite for culture; some—the great majority—with disgust and often bitter hostility. Reymont despises the ruthless slave-driving of Bucholz and Kessler as much as he hates the greediness of Mendelsohn, Grünspan and Grosglik. Reymont's attitude toward the industrial tycoons is never expressed explicitly, but his description of them as being ugly and physically repulsive or machinelike makes it clear. Herman Bucholz, for instance, "dragged himself heavily, leaning on a heavy stick and, bent almost in two, raised his round, red, hawklike eyes and his big, shining round face adorned with small whiskers and a straight mustache." In Bucholz's opinion, Borowiecki, when he was director of his paint shop, was nothing but "the best machine

in this department," although he had a certain liking for the
young engineer and, as Reymont ironically remarks, "even more,
he was worth the whole 10,000 rubles he was being paid."[3]
Himself inhuman, autocratic, and cruel, Bucholz meets his death
in his own factory, surrounded by roaring machines and terrified workers; his last pitiful outcry disappears into the noise
of the factory, more powerful than human destinies. The end of
Bucholz's career once more suggests a comparison with American literature, namely the similar ending of Frank Norris's *The
Octopus* (1901) in which the cruel tycoon Behrman drowns in
the wheat he has gained by ruining the farmers.

Even in their private lives the tycoons cannot live without
fraud. After a moving moment of prayer, Szaja Mendelsohn
pays off two ritual cantors who had assisted him, and says:

"Here, Mendel, a ruble for you!" He gave him a silver coin, and
the cantor began to examine it carefully at the window. "Look here,
it is a genuine ruble. And you, Abraham, will get only seventy-five
kopecks. You did not feel like singing today, you only pretended
to sing. Do you want to deceive me and the Lord?"[4]

Obviously, Reymont was not free of prejudice, but he did
try to treat all groups objectively. Among the Poles in *The
Promised Land* many are either as ruthless as the big businessmen of other nationalities or are pitifully ignorant, passive, lazy,
and unable to adjust to the new industrial environment. The
law of the jungle, which governs life in Lodz, condemns and
destroys these without mercy. Ironically, the only Polish character who has a chance to succeed is Stach Wilczek (whose name
means "the little wolf") whose appetite for power grows with
every small success he achieves through fraud. For Borowiecki,
who having abandoned his fiancée and married Müller's daughter, finally reaches his goal and becomes rich; but his financial
success becomes moral failure.

Since money makes all the difference in the city jungle, every
means to get it is justified. At a family gathering of the Grün-
spans, to force young Albert into bankruptcy to save the family
business, for instance, the gist of the family's argument is, "Don't
be stupid and stand on honesty. Big money is involved." A

popular method for industrialists of "balancing the account" is
to set the factory ablaze to collect insurance on the damage—
a method so common that it appears almost legitimate. Although
those who do not conform to such unwritten laws are either
rejected or considered stupid and inefficient by the successful
characters, Reymont shows the futility of that merciless pursuit
of money. Some of the magnificent palaces in the shadow of the
factories remain empty, merely a shell of social status and wealth.
In others, boredom envelops overdecorated walls and Persian
rugs. Others are a background for wild orgies in which alcohol
and sex are elevated to the highest value. Some have a social
life made absurd by gossip and shallow vanity. Reymont clearly
presents his own point of view in presenting the events in a
bitterly satirical tone.

Such futile efforts to gain happiness by getting rich are epitomized in the story of Borowiecki. After his marriage to the
millionaire's daughter at the end of the novel, he concludes: "I
have gambled away my own happiness. Now I can only create
it for others," but this rather hollow optimism is unconvincing.[5]
A casual meeting with his former fiancée, who has devoted her
life to charity and educating children, cannot really have changed
Borowiecki's drive toward financial success, and the pessimistic
tone of the novel cannot be altered by such a superficial ending.
In a world of ruthless competition, supported by violence and
fraud, Reymont could not see any substantial hope for the
future, neither the future of his protagonists, nor of the society
becoming rapidly industrialized.

III   A Changing Society

Measured by modern social standards, the picture of Lodz
in The Promised Land lacks at least one group: the workers.
The Marxist critics who accuse Reymont of neglecting the pro-
letarians and their role in the "class struggle" ignore the fact
that the first serious labor strikes in Lodz occurred in 1892, while
the novel, as it can be guessed from a casual mention of Victor
Hugo's death as contemporary, takes place in 1885. It is true
that Reymont gave minimal attention to the plight of the working

masses, but the problems of the masses lay outside of his main interest in the capitalists and technical intelligentsia. The workers, when they appear, are treated *en masse,* as an object. Having focused on those who made Lodz a modern inferno, Reymont presented the toiling masses as a magma which the city molded into hazy, gloomy shapes moving in the background against which the industrial Moloch rose to its gigantic dimensions. This focus is particularly evident in the street scenes, where the crowd is used as scenery for the foreground characters; the crowd is drawn so vividly that one can almost feel it, hear it, and even distinguish its forms of speech, but it remains a background. The masses are an elementary force as well, a force which contrasts with the evil power of industry. The use of the masses as an object illustrates Reymont's technique of creating an image to serve as a vehicle for his point of view, a technique which this passage from the last chapter of the novel illustrates:

From distant plains, from the mountains, from remote villages, from capitals and towns, from huts and palaces, from heights and gutters, people pressed on in an endless procession to that "promised land." They came to fertilize it with their own blood, they brought to it their power, youth, health, their freedom, their hopes and misfortunes, brains and labor, faith and dreams.

For that "promised land," for that octopus, the villages have been deserted, the forests have disappeared, the land has been despoiled of its treasures, the rivers dried out. For that land people were born. And it sucked everything in, crushed it in its powerful jaws, and chewed people and objects, the sky and the earth, in return giving useless millions to a handful of people and hunger and hardship to the whole throng.[6]

The anaphoric enumeration renders an uninterrupted slow movement of masses toward the central point, the city, defined in an impressive metaphor which becomes more expressive with every consecutive sentence until the dramatic effect and the author's conclusion have been fully achieved. We shall return to Reymont's style; it is enough at this point merely to indicate the stylistic devices which create the powerful vision and the essential idea of *The Promised Land.*

Some subplots, scenes, and even passages clearly testify less figuratively to Reymont's concern with social problems. A simple story of two peasants who came to Borowiecki for help only to become the victims of "the octopus" instead, is sharply contrasted with the story of Wilczek, who also comes from their village. Although Wilczek is a minor character, he is significant for Reymont's views about a society in transition. Appearing late in the novel, he slowly attains the dimensions of a symbolic figure. By a series of clever transactions, he rises from a job as a minor clerk to social prominence and financial power, and by the end of the novel, to a full-fledged partnership with Baum. Wilczek represents not only a voracious appetite for money but also an even greater energy, one which can match that of the Germans and Jews. A prototype of a new kind of Polish peasant, he is an upstart, in the tradition of Balzac; in the symbolic climax of the first volume Wilczek seems predestined to take the place of the millionaire Bucholz, whose funeral he has just attended. Walking along the streets of Lodz, he sees himself as an inheritor of Bucholz's power:

He loved that "promised land" as a predatory animal loves the wild jungle full of prey. He adored that "promised land" flowing with gold and blood, he desired it, craved it; toward it he extended his greedy arms and cried out with a voice of victory, the voice of hunger: "Mine! Mine!" And there were moments he felt that, had he possessed it for ever, he would not let his loot go until he had sucked all the gold out of it.[7]

No matter how morally repulsive he is, Wilczek is one of the most powerful—and terrifying—characters in Polish literature, testifying to Reymont's insight into the dark soul of the human beast. In this respect the author of *The Promised Land* can stand comparison not only with the masters of Naturalistic novels, Zola and Dreiser, but also with the best authors of Gothic and modern psychological fiction as well.

As if to show that he was capable of understanding also a quite different mode of human behavior, Reymont interwove into the novel a subplot concerning the Jaskolski family, written in rather sentimentally.[8] The Jaskolskis, living in utter poverty, represent those who could not adjust to the new conditions of

urban life. Uprooted from their native land and deprived of
their small fortune, they retained all the pride and prejudices of
the gentry. When offered a job as a night watchman, the old
gentleman Jaskolski replies in anger: "Jaskolski may starve,
but he never will be a watchdog for the Krauts." As a result,
he and his family suffer tragically. For them, as for many others
who met tragedy during that transition period in Polish society,
honor is more important to a gentleman than survival. Reymont, who came from peasant stock himself, refrained from
irony and criticism, and instead showed compassion in his
presentation of their sad plight.

Even more compassionate is the presentation of Dr. Wysocki,
an idealistic physician who is mainly concerned with improving
the social conditions of the workers. Wysocki visits his patients
in the slums, and thus acts as a guide through the lower depths
of human misery. That Wysocki foreshadows one of the most
memorable figures in Polish literature, Dr. Judym in Stefan
Zeromski's novel *Homeless People* (1900), once more shows
Reymont's acute sensitivity to the problems which were to
dominate Polish social life and literature at the turn of the
century.

We have already noticed Reymont's close connection with
Polish literary tradition and his susceptibility to the new trends
emerging in the 1890's. There is, however, in *The Promised
Land* a special group of characters who symbolize the past and,
accordingly, they are depicted in the traditional novelistic form
in a unity of meaning with appropriate stylistic devices which
was Reymont's important contribution to modern fiction. After
the powerful climax of the first volume of the novel, the second
opens in a completely different setting, at the country estate
of Kurow, where Borowiecki and Baum visit for a short vacation.
Because Kurow is soon to be sold, an aura of despair hangs
over their brief idyll. To emphasize the contrast between the
visitors and the residents who are relics of times past, Reymont
imitates the techniques of description and characterization of
Henryk Sienkiewicz, whose historical novels also reflect a
bygone world, that of the seventeenth century Polish nobility.
Julian Krzyzanowski, whose study concentrates on "exploring

in Reymont's work those ties which connect him with Polish literary tradition,"[9] establishes his relationship to Sienkiewicz and others beyond any doubt and credits Reymont with enlivening and changing that tradition. Creating the multicolored, original canvas of *The Promised Land,* the author brought together the best of the older literary heritage with new methods, arranging them according to his own creative vision. The result is a highly original modern composition which reflects the changes taking place in his society.

IV   The Problems of Style

Reymont was already distinguished as a writer with a highly individual style on the basis of such stories as "The Pilgrimage to Jasna Gora," even before writing *The Promised Land.* His first two novels were less impressive stylistically, primarily because he was more concerned with plotting. But in *The Promised Land* Reymont emerged as a mature novelist, in full control of his technique and able to employ it in a major novel of ambitious scope. This novel contains all the characteristics of his later style, brought to a more perfect and sophisticated level in *The Peasants.*

One mark of Reymont's style, accurate depiction of detail, is rooted in his unusual ability to perceive the world around him and to retain whatever he encountered. Grzymala-Siedlecki recalls a casual meeting with Reymont during which he closed his eyes and recalled in the most minute detail the characteristic features of the passers-by and the surroundings, demonstrating an incredible accuracy.[10] Reymont also possessed a talent for mimicry, a talent perhaps stemming from his associations with the theater. He acted out characters and situations by "enlarging his gestures," as Siedlecki put it. Alfred Wysocki, who spent several years with Reymont in Paris, relates a story of Reymont's acting out a bank robbery that he had read about for friends in a café with such vividness that the alarmed owner almost called the police, absolutely convinced that the foreigner must have been involved in a real crime.[11] Added to these talents was an all-embracing curiosity, a curiosity attested to by his friends as well as revealed by the variety of subjects explored in his fiction. But, as the prominent Polish critic Antoni Potocki once remarked, "curiosity about life cannot suffice by itself; an impeccable taste must select from that often abundant richness of detail."[12]

Reymont had both. In the novel, which deals primarily with contemporary material, Reymont's ability to observe was of major importance, while his method of selecting detail and transforming reality into artistic imagery elevated it to art. Brought up in the tradition of Realism with strong tendencies toward Naturalism, Reymont wanted to present reality objectively, but at the same time, he found it necessary to shape his material in new ways to suit his artistic intentions. Reymont's style, then, both reflects the prevailing literary tendencies of the turn of the century and radically departs from them, and in his departures, he is very much a twentieth century novelist.

A major characteristic of the twentieth century novel is the disappearance of the author. Up to the mid-nineteenth century, a novelist intruded frequently into his story, commenting on events, anticipating the fate of characters, and digressing at will. In *The Promised Land,* Reymont has disappeared behind the story, so to speak, letting the characters act and move by themselves, letting the plot develop as if uncontrolled. In the way he handles point of view, Reymont shares the tendency of the Realistic novelists. But in his techniques of plotting, Reymont departs from them. While the masters of the "new school of fiction"—Turgenev, Flaubert, and Henry James—concentrate their plots on a few central characters who are followed closely through crucial events in their lives, Reymont uses characters only to support a controlling image. He neglects the plot in order to focus on his image of the city, and uses his major characters and the amorphous masses to render the spirit and atmosphere of that city. What plotting exists in *The Promised Land* is only the barest minimum essential for the progress of action, and is subservient to the image of Lodz.

Reymont is closest to the Naturalists in his choice of animal imagery and in his use of the premises of social Darwinism. The fate of individuals, the movement of the masses, and their

mutual impact are depicted according to the Darwinian idea
of natural selection in the struggle for survival. His emphasis
on the problems of failure and the futility of the struggle suggests the inherent conflict between the Naturalists' attempts at
impartiality in their view of social evils and human weaknesses
and their basic premises about the human condition. This is
clearly evident in his presentation of the industry, in particular
the machines achieving supernatural dimensions.

Reymont's highly metaphorical language often is drawn from
the vocabulary of the biological sciences, particularly zoology
and entomology. Factories are referred to as beasts, monsters,
octopuses, spiders, and the like, in order to reveal their inhuman
and apocalyptic qualities, especially when the machines have
bcome a threat to the fate of men. Reymont often expands such
metaphors, multiplying the basic associative idea, as he does,
for example, with a factory whistle in the opening paragraph of
The Promised Land.

The first shrill whistle of a factory pierced the silence of the early
morning, and in all parts of the city the others began to rise, following
it more and more noisily, and they screamed with their hoarse, unruly
voices like a choir of monstrous roosters crowing with their metal
throats a signal to work.[13]

The metaphor is continued even further in the next paragraph,
in which the factories take on animal forms—they have carcasses
and necks—and even "wake up" and "breathe"; the factories
"begin to live and move." The effect of the increasing humanization of the factories is the decreasing humanization of men.
Similar images occur on almost every page, wherever the author
describes the city and especially at the tense moments in which
the factories assume human activities. A machine devours two
human antagonists who are fighting in front of it; Borowiecki's
factory suddenly blows up, requiting him for his unfaithfulness,
consuming his labors and hopes in its flames; a locomotive pull-
ing Borowiecki to that fire is first a "steed set with spurs,"
and later, when hope for saving the factory is lost, becomes a
"giant beetle." Here, as elsewhere, Reymont uses the device

of the pathetic fallacy—endowing inanimate objects with human emotions.

These few examples also indicate another quality of Reymont's style—highly emotional diction. He "enlarged his gestures" in literature as well as in life. He often replaces denotative terms with synonyms of a higher connotative intensity, which are, unfortunately, often untranslatable because of the way in which Reymont uses the possibilities of inflection in Polish to create new, more emotional forms of words. This characteristic of his style reached its ultimate development in *The Peasants*, which Maria Rzeuska describes as "making an impression of giantism, multiplicity, and theatrical pathos of presentation," and which she calls by an apt term, "maximalism."[14] Such characteristics of imagery and diction play an ever-increasing role in Reymont's work; in *The Promised Land* they are introduced for the first time as an outstanding stylistic feature and their presence is part of the reason for the significance of that novel in Reymont's creative development.

Equally important are his dialogues. While the emotional diction of the descriptive passages creates a sense of the author's subjective opinions, the impersonal tone of the dialogues returns the novel to objectivity and the author to the background, and keeps the whole in a stylistic balance. Reymont allows his characters to speak for themselves. Compared with his previous work, the dialogue in *The Promised Land* demonstrates Reymont's increasing skill. Each social group, almost each character, has highly individualized speech. Only the intelligentsia use standard, educated Polish, although Borowiecki, an engineer, often uses German technical expressions or the jargon of the *"Lodzer-Menschen,"* especially in business matters. It is interesting to note, however, that while Borowiecki, whose language is otherwise correct, uses German technical terms, an English specialist in the same factory, Mr. Murray, speaks flawless Polish without any traces of either English or German. There seems to be a reason for that inconsistency of linguistic characterization. Very often in the novel, the more unpleasant a character, the less colorful his linguistic representation. We may assume that the novelist did not consider such characters important enough to

endow them with speech characterization which would make
them stand out of the crowd. This, however, applies mostly for
the Poles in the novel.

The Germans in *The Promised Land* are linguistically far more
interesting. They either speak incorrect Polish, confusing gen-
ders and cases (*Pan zna moja Wilhelm?*) or insert German
words into Polish sentences (*Ten Müller jest jeszcze zupelnie
jugend*). But again, psychologically rather colorless Max Baum
does not distinguish himself with any special features in his
speech except a few dialectic expressions (*pozarlem sie z fatrem*)
commonly used by Polonized Germans. Even at his home, a
typical German family, perfect Polish is used by everyone except
one likable character, a grandmother. Reymont uses foreign
words, then, as a stylistic device emphasizing a character's personality, making him more colorful and often funny. The latter
quality is particularly evident in his treatment of the Jews, whose
language in *The Promised Land* is so interesting and ingenious
it deserves a chapter by itself.

The Jewish population in Poland tended to preserve its own
language and customs, including its way of living, dress, and
social habits based on religion and tradition. In most communities
Jews lived in open ghettos, hardly mixing with their neighbors.
But in a big industrial city such as Lodz, where most of the
banking, financing, and trade was in Jewish hands, there was
inevitably an interrelationship between Jews and other inhabitants, which tended to overcome the numerous traditional boundaries depicted earlier in the novel *Meir Ezofowicz* (1878) by
the Polish novelist Eliza Orzeszkowa. In Lodz, Yiddish tended to
mix with Polish in a peculiar blend, a new industrial jargon
saturated with technical terms; it was widely used among
businessmen who had to adjust to the new society, even at the
expense of their own tradition, no matter whether it was Jewish
or Polish. Reymont showed various problems of that process of
adaptation in many scenes and aspects all through the novel.
"The golden youth," for example, young men and girls from
wealthy families gathering at Roza Mendelsohn's are seemingly
indifferent to national and cultural boundaries; however, as
soon as one of them, Mela Grünspan, falls in love with Dr.

Wysocki, the illusion disappears and the two cultures become incompatible again.

The differences between the two national groups are also rendered linguistically. Although the Jews in the novel speak Polish, not Yiddish, their language is heavily tainted with often grotesque syntactic and verbal inaccuracies. The effect is often humorous, never malicious, since Reymont's anger—when expressed by his characterizations—is directed against unscrupulous methods in business and not against the Jews or Germans as nationalities. Incompatible similes and the repetition of interrogative sentences are characteristic of his rendering of the Jewish manner of speaking:

"Is it true that cotton went up?"
"What does it mean it went up? It jumps like a locomotive, it soars like a balloon, for it doesn't care that Lodz might break its neck."[15]

Satirical as he is in presenting the upper classes of the Jewish society, as for instance in the scene of a party at the Edelmans, where paintings are being displayed and discussed as material values rather than works of art, Reymont was also fully aware of more serious problems in the national life, especially economic questions. As usual in the novel these problems are presented in the form of artistic images interwoven into the main plot. When, for instance, Moryc Welt walks along the streets in Lodz, he reads the signs displayed in front of the stores:

"Lipa, Chaskiel Cokolwiek, Ita Aronsohn, Josef Reinberg," etc., etc., only Jewish names, once in a while threaded with some German names. "Our people only," he whispered with some sort of relief, and a contemptuous smile appeared on his lips and shone in his eyes when he saw a Polish name on a little sign at a shoemaker's or a locksmith's.[16]

In general, however, Reymont did not emphasize the economic differences later known as the so-called "Jewish problem"—one of the most likeable figures in *The Peasants* is a Jewish innkeeper—but concentrated rather on individual characters and tried to make them as real as possible, no matter what their nationality, creed, or social status. This was an objectivity rising above the prejudices of his epoch.

The linguistic characterization then contributes to the novel's style, and, at the same time, marks an important step in Reymont's own method of writing, more diversified and versatile than in any of his previous novels and short stories.

V A Modern Novel

The Promised Land played a crucial role in Reymont's creative development as well as in the history of Polish literature. Although it has never been known well enough to have much effect on the development of fiction, it deserves a significant place in the history of European novel for extraliterary reasons as well as literary. Julian Krzyzanowski, relating *The Promised Land* to Ruskin's theories of the destructive role of industrialization in modern society, observes:

Thanks to them [Ruskin's theories] *The Promised Land*, without the author's knowledge or will, has become a single large artistic painting in European literature which realizes Ruskin's moral postulates, and at the same time, thanks to the primitive nature of the workers' lives depicted on its pages, it has become a valuable historical document in which the artist fixed forever the outlines of a relationship soon to disappear completely as a result of radical changes in the situation of the European worker.[17]

Despite a certain overstatement—the situation of the workers occupies only a minor place in the novel—the novelist did create an uniquely modern novel about the problems of industrialization and its effects on all of society rather than on an individual protagonist, and he found his own artistic idiom to solve that new and singular problem. Especially worth stressing is Reymont's inventive structure which easily carries his broad vision of a society confused in its attempts to adjust to the age of industrialization and technology.

The plot, negligible compared to that in the traditional nineteenth century work, is still sufficient to sustain the action of a multitude of highly diversified characters. The novel thus avoids the danger of becoming a social treatise and develops, instead, according to the laws of fiction. Accurate description, powerful imagery, and vivid dialogue contribute to the richness without weakening the novel's sociological, almost documentary, character. In short, the artistic technique suits the modern subject. With this novel Reymont introduced a new type of fiction, which was to develop further in the twentieth century.

VI *"On a Certain Day"*

Although such a large canvas as *The Promised Land* has room enough for practically every aspect of life in a modern city, certain of Reymont's attitudes did not fit his conception. Later, when he better perceived the new trends in Polish literature—particularly the Symbolism and Neo-Romanticism of the first decade of the new century—Reymont grew more and more aware that a totally Realistic method could not render adequately many problems of the human psyche. One of them fascinated the novelist in particular, namely the complex psychological relationship between men and machines. This problem, to be one of the later issues of Futurism and related literary movements, Reymont saw early and attempted to solve through the use of symbols, which found its fullest expression in two novelettes, "The Cemetery" (1908) and *Bunt* (The Riot) (1924).

In *The Promised Land,* the memorable image of the city as an octopus is a forerunner of that new attitude. The author's attention, however, was devoted mostly to the Moloch-like city and the passive masses of people whom it devours and destroys, not to the problems of the individual who faces the monster of industry. In numerous passages, to be sure, the machines seem to possess almost complete control over human beings, but in most cases their control is over their bodies, not their souls. Later Reymont explored the psychological aspects in a symbolic short story "On a Certain Day" (1900), which supplements the novel and also anticipates his essentially new attitude toward industrialization and urban communities.

The story is structured on a twofold contrast between man and machine, on the one hand, and on the other, between city and countryside—the contrast implied in the scene at Kurow in

The Promised Land. The setting plays a symbolic role in the one-day experience of Mr. Pliszka, whose very name, "a wagtail" in Polish, symbolizes his helplessness and weakness. A former soldier, who resembles the memorable Mr. Rzecki in Prus's *The Doll,* Pliszka has run an elevator in a factory for twenty years. "He had become the oldest machine in the factory, just a machine, since he began slowly to forget about himself, his life, and there were moments when he did not know anymore who he once was and where."[18] It is interesting to compare this passage with a similar one about Borowiecki: while Bucholz considers him a machine, he is an important, though impersonal, part of the factory. Pliszka is a mere object, a passive, automatic part of a bigger machine. The author's attitude about the role of the individual in industrialized society has clearly changed.

Pliszka's ego fades away, and like a robot he works in his elevator without a single thought of his own until a certain fine day in May, when he suddenly becomes aware of the existence of a world outside the factory walls. Having overheard a conversation among some workers who had gone home for the week-end, Pliszka begins to dream about the fields and the woods, reviving old memories in his fancy. After a long struggle with his fears and with his slavish attachment to the factory, he decides to visit the countryside. This visit is followed by a firm decision to escape the bondage of factory life. But when Pliszka finally leaves the city, he has to face something besides the suddenly rediscovered beauty of nature: he confronts the meaning of time and its effect on himself and on the country, fondly cherished in his memories. Standing at the threshold of freedom, Pliszka thinks he hears the whistle of his factory calling him back to duty, and he obeys it. He abandons the dream, overpowered by fears of the reality.

The juxtaposition between the demonic power of the factory and the delicate charm of nature is further emphasized because it takes place in a simple human soul. In Pliszka's imagination the factory really is calling him back. It has such a strong hold over him that when he cries, he does so "silently in fear that the machines might overhear his complaint."

Thus the dilemma of the "little man" in the modern world, which Chaplin later epitomized, Reymont made into a simple human story revealing a man's fears in the face of dangers he felt instinctively but did not yet fully realize. On that note Reymont closed another chapter in his artistic development.

CHAPTER 5

Before The Peasants

I *Early Short Stories*

THUS far our discussion of Reymont's works has been thematic rather than chronological, reserving for further analysis the short stories and sketches preceding *The Peasants* but which belong thematically to the same cycle. He wrote in a series of thematic cycles usually including several sketches and short stories and eventually each resulted in major works. *The Comedienne* crowned the theatrical cycle, for instance, and *The Promised Land*, the urban. In the peasant cycle, therefore, the early stories of peasant life provide valuable material for a better understanding of the creative method which culminated in Reymont's prize-winning novel, *The Peasants*.

Reymont and his family were deeply rooted in country life. From early childhood Reymont observed the Polish countryside and its inhabitants, growing up in communion with nature and the land. His inborn talent to perceive and retain minute details helped him remember those years accurately throughout his life and it was in France where Adam Mickiewicz wrote his epic poem *Pan Tadeusz* (1834) that Reymont did most of his work on *The Peasants*. Each of these two writers apparently needed to be removed from immediate political pressures, in order to achieve perspective on their native land. The resulting two works, a poem and a novel, are hardly surpassed by any works in their respective genres in Polish literature.

Before going abroad, Reymont explored his subject in several short stories, largely based on experiences and impressions gathered when he lived among the peasants in Lipce and Krosnowa between 1889 and 1893. Collected into a volume published in 1897, after his first two novels, these stories chiefly deal with

64

the peasants and their life in the country. Two of the stories, "The Death" and "Tomek Baran," deserve detailed discussion because they reveal once more Reymont's constant quest for appropriate artistic methods and his experimentation with various literary techniques.

"The Death," written in 1891 and first published in 1893, may well serve as a document of the Naturalistic method adopted by the author at that early stage of his literary career. Undoubtedly one of the most cruel stories in Polish literature, "The Death" resembles in tone the grim bestiality and ruthlessness reflected in the stories of Zola and Maupassant, whose influence was quite strong in Polish letters during that period. The human beast appears naked in "The Death," driven by a single force, the desire to possess. To the peasants, possession naturally meant land, and so the characters in "The Death" resolve to commit the most horrible crime, a parricide, in order to satisfy their hunger for land. The author obviously understood peasant motives of behavior very well and chose an effective way to show it in action.

The story focuses on the death of an old man. Having divided his land between his two daughters, he spends his last days at the house of one of them, Antkowa. Because she is deeply envious of her sister who received more land, in an outburst of violent anger, Antkowa chases her father away to freeze to death in a barn among the pigs and cows. The death, followed by a family fight and the funeral, is marked by animalistic passion and violence. In this story Reymont not only proved to be an apt student of his Naturalistic masters but also able to set action into a realistically presented situation and to create a dense atmosphere of drama with the simplest possible artistic devices. His characters, dramatic and reaching the depths of ancient tragedy, are strikingly vivid and real in their actions, their behavior, even the dialect of their speech. At the same time, they achieve almost universal dimensions thanks to the truthfulness of their psychological motivation. Their inhumanity reveals the darkest side of human character.

A Polish critic, Lech Budrecki, offers a Marxist interpretation of the story as "a picture of moral disintegration caused by in-

human conditions in a capitalistic society" and "a commercial-
ization of passions,"[1] but such a reading offers just a limited
interpretation. What is of real interest in the story is its deep
insight into the psychology and motives of Antkowa on the one
hand, and Reymont's method of presentation on the other. A
careful reading of the story shows that the author achieved a
penetrating understanding of the people who were to become
the subject of his major novel. That understanding resulted in
compassion and, eventually, a feeling of responsibility for revealing their ordeals to the world. Literature in Poland has always
been motivated by a writer's awareness of a special mission,
either patriotic or social, while the artistic shape of his work
has often been considered of secondary importance. It took
Reymont years to free himself from that tradition, although
he lived in a period when more emphasis was placed on artistic than on extraliterary values.

The function of a writer as a fighter, or at least as a representative of an issue, is also apparent in "Tomek Baran" (1894).
The story explores the psychological problem of an unemployed
worker whose tragedy is presented against the rich background
of peasant life. The realistic presentation of poverty and the
internal tensions of a small rural community emphasize Tomek's
dilemma—how to survive without a job and money. Accused of
stealing, he has lost his job at the railroad. When the story begins,
his only consolation for a hopeless situation is to spend his last
kopecks on vodka.

This setting gives the author an opportunity to sketch a series
of minor characters and to insert some local color, such as a
peasant dance accompanied by a song in couplets. Some of these
characters, incidentally, will reappear in a more fully developed
form in The Peasants, and the motif of dancing will return in the
novel in famous passages which have been considered masterpieces of Reymont's descriptive style. "Tomek Baran," then,
should be considered as an early sketch for the novel, or at least
as an introduction to one of its peasant motifs which remained
in the author's mind until they found a completely perfected
form.

The story is much more than a study of peasants; it explores certain social problems intelligently and penetratingly. Unemployment, poverty, and the hunger of the peasants are often dramatically juxtaposed with the wealth of those of higher social status, as in the scene when Tomek comes to the parish office to beg for help. He is received by the priest whose portrayal is a real satiric masterpiece. Although the priest does not hide his compassion for the poor man, he is more than reluctant to give generously. Instead, he delivers a little sermon about the financial difficulties of the Pope and with every new phrase he withdraws coins from the small sum of money he had intended to give. We shall meet this priest again in *The Peasants,* a complex and realistic character driven by human passions, as ready to burst out with curses as with blessings, more concerned with his own household than his parish, yet sincerely loving his "little souls," who repay his prayers with fresh eggs and tender chickens.

Even though Reymont's satiric method becomes stronger in the scene of Tomek's encounter with the railroad officials whom he begs for another job, he continues to treat his protagonist, Tomek, as a tragic figure. Rejected and humiliated, he returns to his hut only to find his son dying of the poisoned meat he had bought a day before. The boy's death, however, brings an ironic change in Tomek's plight. Moved by his tragedy, the neighbors come one by one, offering food and supplies from their own modest lot; they save Tomek and his remaining children.

This expression of social solidarity especially enraged the Marxist critics, who denounced Reymont for praising this solidarity while totally neglecting the "class struggle" in that story. For Reymont, however, despite differences in social position and wealth, a community was cemented together with strong human bonds. Fully aware of social stratification, he nevertheless stressed those elements which tied a peasant to the land and explored the common factors which united them as a special type of people. It is true that later, in *The Peasants,* the differences between the peasants and other classes came to the foreground in the form of various economic conflicts, but even there the beggar Agata and the richest farmer in Lipce, Boryna, still belong to the same community and are moved by common problems.

Reymont's early stories are thus of paramount importance. He emerged as the first Polish writer to be thoroughly familiar with the peasants and their life, and he introduced them as a new and major subject in Polish literature at a time when the power of the peasants as a social group was the new emerging factor in Polish national life. At the turn of the century, they suddenly began to represent new hope for a nation divided among three foreign powers. With the increasing organization and importance of the peasant movement, that part of the nation, oppressed and neglected for centuries, became the very focus of political and cultural life. In 1895 an official political party, *Stronnictwo Ludowe* (The Peasant Party), was organized. The increasing role of that new social force found artistic ramification in literature, painting, and music.

From being the subject of only marginal sketches and stories by the major writers in the nineteenth century, the peasants moved to a prominent place in literature and became the subject of novels and plays of major artistic significance. They occupy a central place in works by Wladyslaw Orkan, Kazimierz Tetmajer, and Stanislaw Wyspianski. In a summary of the historical development of the peasant as a subject in Polish literature Julian Krzyzanowski concludes:

At the turn of the century came the proper moment to take an epic outlook at the Polish peasant, just as seventy years before *Pan Tadeusz* had captured the last glimmerings of the ancient life of the gentry slowly turning into the new life of the intelligentsia. And, as at that time that task was realized by Mickiewicz, now it became the job of Reymont, the writer who all through his previous career was predestined for it.[2]

II   *"Righteously"*

The peasant theme grew stronger and stronger throughout Reymont's early works, gradually capturing his major attention. From the short story it was expanded into a novelette, *Sprawie-dliwie* (Righteously), written in 1899, after *The Promised Land.* This should be considered, Ignacy Matuszewski remarked, as "in a way the prologue to *The Peasants,* in which Reymont applied his ability gained by experience to a theme of great scope, and found a truly epic tone."[3]

Having achieved a considerable success with his three novels, Reymont was most ready to cope with the topic now occupying his creative mind, but he approached it cautiously, first as a novelette, and only two years later as a full-scale novel. Larger in size, more ambitious, and better structured than the previous stories and sketches, the novelette surpassed them in breadth of presentation of the peasants' life. A close examination of "Righteously" discloses many elements later developed in the peasant novel, and even some motifs which the author intended to elaborate on in a sequel to *The Peasants*, which he never wrote.

The story centers seemingly on a young man, Jasiek Winciorek, who, having escaped from prison, returns to his native village and makes plans to join a group of emigrants to America. In fact, however, "Righteously" is a thorough study of a whole community and its reaction to Jasiek's fate. A wide variety of characters and subplots even if only remotely related to the main plot are indispensable to the full projection of the multiple facets of life in a rural community. All of these characters—the head of the village, the innkeeper, travelling beggars, the priest and the squire—provide as much background for the story as the masterly descriptions of landscape, which results in a complete picture of a typical Polish village at the end of the nineteenth century. Characteristic scenes, such as that of a child's birth or of the office of a local clerk, are interwoven with discussions on social and economic questions in the community's day-to-day life. They all merge into unity with the main plot, enriching it and contributing to the progress of the action. Reymont had practiced the structural techniques used here before, but here they are completely mastered in a compact, well-organized composition.

The dramatic progress of the story is enhanced by the mounting tension as the Russian authorities, continuously referred to only as "the watchmen" (Reymont was trying to avoid political implications in order to by-pass the occupier's censorship), organize a search for Jasiek and with every day follow closer on his tracks. The tension reaches its climax when Jasiek misses the departure of the party illegally crossing the border to emigrate to the United States; instead he meets a group of peasants ordered by the head of the village to round him up. After a short fight Jasiek escapes, and with his last furious strength, he sets the village ablaze. Captured by his persecutors, he must meet a terrible punishment: they throw him into the flames in the presence of his mother. Before dying of a stroke, she whispers: "Righteously." She recognizes Jasiek's unbelievable crime against the community. In the words of Matuszewski, "the solidarity with her own social group, which the reckless incendiary violated, prevails over maternal instincts."[4]

Thus the community takes precedence over the individual although both are inseparably mingled as later, in *The Peasants,* the personal fate of Boryna is joined with the life of Lipce. In his previous novels Reymont focused on either the protagonist or a group, but in this story the protagonist and the group receive equal attention, creating an artistic unity.

Reymont mastered also two more important elements of fiction in "Righteously," the art of description and the use of colloquial language. In the early novels descriptions of nature had been interjected into the main plot, sometimes being loosely related to the action, more often creating an atmosphere or a mood charged with symbolic meaning as in *The Promised Land.* In "Righteously" descriptions form an intrinsic part of the plot, and are kept in balance with the action. From the inn in which he finds a brief refuge Jasiek escapes into the forest, only to find himself surrounded by his own fears, taking on the shapes of the trees; later, when he falls asleep exhausted from terror, the same forest "became silent, leaned over the sleeping one, and stood as if keeping a very alert watch, protecting him from the rain."[5] Nature here takes part, as it were, in the action, enters it actively and cannot be separated from Jasiek's story. Moreover, the protagonist becomes part of nature and experiences its protection. This feeling of a complete communion with nature and landscape becomes so overwhelming that Jasiek cannot make up his mind to emigrate. Later in the story nature forms a background which enhances the presentation of Jasiek's experiences. For instance, one of the most memorable love scenes Reymont ever wrote takes place under the blooming trees of an orchard and has for a climax a prayer as the Angelus bell resounds over the distant fields. This makes the contrast of the dramatic ending all the more powerful. For Jasiek's crime is more than just an outburst of personal violence—it violates the law of Nature by turning against the eternal order which, in spite of tensions, prevails over the village.

The style of descriptions in "Righteously" also marks a decisive step forward. Masterly as they are, the descriptions in such earlier stories as "The Blizzard" and "The Bitch" are purely pictorial. In "Righteously" we not only see but also sense and feel the environment:

At sunset the weather cleared up completely, a slight frost began to set in; cold, gray, thin fog began to settle on the fields, and after the sunset the sky was covered with purple scales and with gulfs filled with blood; the mud set quickly and strained under feet like leather straps. The sharp smell of frost mixed with raw smell of oak-leaves decaying in the woods, and sometimes the smell of smoke borne by the fog.[6]

The three-dimensional perception places the reader within the image and makes all his senses aware of nature and the landscape which Reymont recreates instead of merely describing. This technique is further perfected in his later works, particularly in *The Peasants* and his historical trilogy.

A colloquial vocabulary and syntax are used extensively to individualize the speech of various characters, a method Reymont had used earlier, but here some phrases in the vernacular are introduced in "seemingly reported speech";[7] that is, Reymont makes use of dialect not only in dialogues but also to reflect the thoughts. Dialect sometimes identifies Reymont's point of view with the character's or, at times, marks a distance between the author and a character or provides an explanatory comment. When the old Winciorkowa laments Jasiek's fate, realizing the impossibility of escape, Reymont identifies himself with her thoughts by using the vernacular Polish expression *laboga* (my God) or *nikaj* (nowhere) instead of the grammatical *dla Boga* and *nigdzie*. In the next paragraph, though, she becomes the object of the author's sympathy with a remark made, as it were, from a distance, indicating the difference between the intellectual level of her simple mind and that of the narrator: "Poor thing, she could not understand that word 'law,' and thought it was the same as 'justice.' "[8]

Reymont also used highly personalized speech to emphasize his satiric treatment of characters like the priest or the squire's wife who, listening to Winciorkowa's lament, "whispered to her husband in French: 'A Niobe! A rustic Niobe,' " and begging the old woman to continue crying, brought a huge camera, "for she was passionately occupied with photography and painting but considered photography more important."[9] Here the striking contrast between real suffering and a superficial reaction is enhanced by the two different forms of speech, which characterize the two women as representatives of two different worlds.

All of these stylistic features, which were for the first time consciously employed in "Righteously" by a mature artist, were carried further in Reymont's next book, his major novel *The Peasants*.

CHAPTER 6

The Peasants

THE first decade of the twentieth century marked a decisive change in Polish literature. Realistic prose gave way to poetry, Naturalism was replaced by Symbolism, and a new period, often called Neo-Romanticism, began. Under the strong influence of French Symbolism, Polish literature replaced the sober, matter-of-fact prose of Realism with new poetic methods for exploring the human soul.

The generation of the realists gave way to the poets and novelists of "Young Poland," who together with the painters, composers, and art theoreticians, either exploited their intimate feelings or followed their spiritual leader, Stanislaw Przybyszewski, in discovering the "naked soul." Their artistic forms were only vaguely related to the Realistic tradition. "Art for art's sake" became the watchword, although recent studies disclose some additional concerns in that seemingly purely esthetic movement. Julian Krzyzanowski in his study of the history of that period stated that "the Neoromantic movement, at least ours, from the very beginning had a clearly social coloring,"[1] and related it to the social and political awakening of the peasants and the growth of the right-wing political program of the emerging National Democratic Party, led by Roman Dmowski. In his philosophy and his literary technique, Reymont was influenced by both the artistic and political developments.

It must have been expected that Reymont, one of the most promising writers of the new generation, would play a significant role in the new developments. Among the writers considered as a link between the old traditions and the new epoch, both he and Stefan Zeromski had entered the new century with literary achievements gained in the 1890's, yet they

were still susceptible to the new trends. Both were distinguished
by a highly emotional, subjective style, which was regarded by
contemporary critics as a vital ingredient of the new fiction;
both were interested in social issues. These two men, connected
by a peculiar fate until they were both later considered for the
Nobel Prize, were often mentioned in the same breath, although
their differences were greater than their similarities. Only in
1925, the year in which they both died, did that unwilling competition end.

By 1902 Reymont's reputation in Polish literature was well
established. Having published three novels and several volumes
of short stories he was generally regarded as a novelist of far-
reaching possibilities who had not yet said his last word and who
was still capable of a major achievement. Reviewing the two
first volumes of *The Peasants*, published in 1902, Matuszewski,
who had been watching Reymont's work from the very beginning,
predicted:

Without closing the files of critical opinion until the second half
of the novel is published, we have every right to suppose because
of what the author has already published that *The Peasants* will
be a work equal to the best in European literature, and at the same
time thoroughly familiar and our own.[2]

Of course, this opinion was based on more than Reymont's
most recent novel. Matuszewski and the other critics recognized
how much Reymont's art had progressed in the past decade and,
therefore, his possibilities for the future. Meanwhile Reymont,
to a great extent remote from literary opinions and discussions,
worked in Paris on the novel, resolved to fulfill the expectations
of the critics and the ever-widening circle of his readers.

Two anecdotes illustrate his lack of concern with literary
gossip and reveal his attitude toward opinion-making coteries.
Alfred Wysocki, who as a young man belonged to the artistic
Bohemia in Cracow, recalls vividly how in 1900, "a young, pale
but exquisitely dressed gentleman" entered a café, and "with
the air of a lord ordered iced coffee, which in our eyes was the
peak of extravagance, and a pack of Egyptian cigarettes." Having
learned that it was Reymont, Wysocki engaged him in conver-

sation and learned that he was undergoing intensive treatment in a local clinic and was engaged in a lawsuit against a railroad company seeking compensation for an accident after which he "could not write as well as he used to." Absolute abstinence from drinking was a part of the treatment which, according to Wysocki, "did not prevent Reymont from buying drinks for his friends and himself many times."[3] The self-confident young author stayed away from company most of the time, nevertheless. He never became part of that group of young men who spent their days and nights in the cafés.

When they met again in Paris, Reymont was working on *The Peasants,* and Wysocki asked why the author did not live in Warsaw or Cracow, where it would have been much more convenient to study his subject. He received a characteristic reply: "There is not such an atmosphere as here. Here everybody is doing something. Life is divided into hours of professional business and relaxation. One can concentrate better and write more easily. I can live here as I want to, and there is no one to disturb me."[4] Obviously, as much as he liked literary cafés, Reymont felt free in Paris from the pressures of social life and professional gossip which would have involved him in Poland; he could concentrate, realizing fully that he was working on his *opus vitae.*

I *An Epic in Prose*

A complex set of factors contributed to the genesis of *The Peasants.* The general public interest in the peasantry was enhanced by the significance they gained from increasing research of folklore, linguistics, and the visual arts. Reymont's own position as an author with a special interest in the peasants had been firmly established by the publication of his short stories, and he was commonly regarded as the "bard of the countryside." Financially independent after his successful suit against the railroad, he could now afford to write a long novel without interruptions over a period of several years. His temporary expatriation also helped him to establish the perspective to explore complex problems from a distance.

He began writing *The Peasants* in Cracow on November 7, 1901, and then, after moving to Paris, finished three volumes by August 18, 1905. Volume four was completed in 1907. The novel was serialized in *Tygodnik Illustrowany* (Illustrated Weekly) between January 1902 and December 1908, and the first editions appeared in 1904, 1906, and 1909, respectively.[5] The first two volumes, *Autumn* and *Winter,* were published together, followed by separate publication of *Spring* in 1906 and *Summer* in 1909. The lapse of time between the latter volumes was due to various circumstances in Reymont's life and bears heavily on the overall composition of the novel.

According to the memoirs of his contemporaries, Reymont worked on the novel very systematically. Lorentowicz recalls that the novelist had a precise outline of the novel and by writing one or two hours every morning produced the finished manuscript from it, without rewriting.[6] Wysocki says that Reymont worked on *Spring* from an outline made "in a notebook with an oilcloth cover, densely covered with writing and marked with blue pencil."[7] Both diarists agree that Reymont was entirely absorbed in his work, quoting many anecdotes to show how little he knew or cared about Paris—after three years there, he was still unaware of the existence of the upper part of Sainte-Chapelle, the main section of that famous church. With his wife Aurelia, whom he had married in Warsaw in 1902, Reymont occupied an apartment at Boulevard du Montparnasse. He seldom went to the theater, read newspapers only occasionally, and confined himself to his Polish friends, such prominent writers as Stefan Zeromski, Zenon Przesmycki, Lucjan Rydel, and Stanislaw Przybyszewski. As the novel progressed, he devoted more and more time to writing, sometimes to the point of exhaustion. Grzymala-Siedlecki tells a story about the novelist during that period. When a physician, who was summoned by Mrs. Reymont who was worried by her husband's poor health, began an examination, Reymont supposedly exclaimed: "What do you want? I have just spent three days dancing at Boryna's wedding." He was referring to a scene in *The Peasants.* Siedlecki concludes that when working, Reymont characteristically lived

his creation: "he himself became each of his characters, personally experiencing the situation he described."[8]

The formidable task of *The Peasants* must have been ex-
hausting indeed. His plan for the novel, intended as a tetralogy
with each volume corresponding to one season, was to present
all aspects of life in the countryside, as regulated by the change
of seasons. Dmitry Cizevskij in his studies in East European
literature and culture often refers to "landwirtschaftliches Jahr,"
the agricultural year, as the basic unit of time among the Slavs,[9]
pointing out its importance even in recent times. This unit of
time provided the author with a structural device to encompass
his treatment of national life, nature, and plot. The conception
was never fully realized, however; the framework proved too
large for his plot to sustain. Some extraliterary reasons contributed to the artistic unevenness of the latter sections of *The
Peasants*, which breaks into two halves; the climax comes at
the end of *Winter*, and the two remaining sections appear to be
padded in places with new and barely relevant subplots and
descriptions. Nevertheless, the novel as a whole has such a
monolithic character that even the weaker parts do not measur-
ably lessen its overall effect.

The structure evoked considerable critical response. We may
dismiss Budrecki's attribution of the difference between the
two halves of the novel to the "ideological crisis" which supposedly resulted in "an end of Reymont's Realism"[10] in the middle of *Spring*. Other critics deserve more attention. Maria Rzeuska
distinguishes at least three functions of the "year scheme" in
The Peasants: the year which brings seasonal change, the yearly
rhythm of a peasant's work in the fields, and the year of the
Catholic ritual.[11] In general Rzeuska correctly equates the epic
character of the novel with the first of these conceptions of time,
which provides the basic structure for the novel. Julian Krzyzanowski, going further, sees the novel as a pure epic and points
out some striking similarities of compositional devices between
The Peasants and works by Homer, Mickiewicz, Sienkiewicz, and
other epic writers. He admits Reymont's originality in the epic
genre and relates it directly to the stylistic devices in the novel.[12]

Against the cycle of the four seasons Reymont unfolds two

main plots, each carrying a multitude of subplots and scenes intrinsically interrelated and interdependent. The stories of the village of Lipce and of the Boryna family are so closely interwoven that it is hard to discuss them as two different plots. In a detailed analysis of this interweaving Rzeuska concludes that the novel is typically epic since "it has many such features and functions that do not represent the main element, the direct goal, but serve mainly as a device, an opportunity to show and unfold a picture of village life."[13] To achieve epic proportions was obviously Reymont's chief concern, for he employed in the novel all the devices characteristic of an epic poem: the parallelism of two plots, nature and society as motivators of the protagonist's behavior, a multitude of events composing the panoramic picture, action slowed by descriptions, style, etc. As a modern novelist, he knew the importance of plot and action in a work of fiction and therefore used devices to hold the reader's interest by introducing, for instance, a love story as an element of intrigue. Curiously enough, he based that love story on a motif derived from *Phaedra*, adding an element of tragedy to the novel's scope.

The marriage of the old Boryna, a wealthy farmer, with a young girl, Jagna, is complicated by the fact that she is in love with Boryna's son, Antek. After marrying Boryna she becomes Antek's stepmother and eventually his mistress. This is clearly the motif of incest, well known since Euripides's play *Hippolytus*. To make the "triangle" even more complicated, Reymont gives a substantial role to a fourth character, Antek's wife, Hanka, who, by remaining morally strong and faithful, represents endurance in overcoming all moral and physical hardships, suffering and humiliation.

Each of these four closely related characters has a different conflict with the others and with the community. Boryna loves his young wife, hates his son for being her lover, but trusts Hanka, in whom he sees a real elemental power. Antek is at odds with everybody: he hates his father for marrying Jagna and for depriving him of inheritance; he cannot stand Hanka because she is an obstacle to his uncontrollable passion for Jagna; and he is unable to forgive Jagna for marrying Boryna—

in fact, at the decisive moment he abandons her completely.
Equally complicated are Hanka's feelings for she loves her
unfaithful husband and is resolved to undergo any hardship
for his sake. She deeply respects Boryna, and feels for Jagna
a peculiar mixture of jealousy and compassion. Jagna, as a symbol of womanhood and passion, moved by forces beyond her
comprehension, marries the old man because she is told to. She is
in love with Antek, but cannot leave her husband; she cannot
endure Hanka's presence, but readily submits to her orders when
they live together at Boryna's. As the action progresses, the relationships among the four become even more complicated.

With his four characters entangled in a tragic relationship,
their pattern of life determined by the four seasons, Reymont
unfolds a conception of life as being regulated by the laws of
all-encompassing nature, which dictates the pace of living, and
creates within human beings uncontrollable love and hatred. It
is nature which dictates the behavior of people who are equally
able to possess and to destroy. Those elemental forces make the
novel a great panorama in which common, everyday existence
in a small Polish village has been heightened to become a universal drama of the human condition. Its basically realistic
conception gives way to a broader and more complex idea.

The novel develops on several levels, saturated with universal
as well as specific meanings. We shall discuss them in a sequence
of aspects in order to explore the full artistic and human value
of *The Peasants*.

II   *The Story of Love and Passion*

Most critics who devote considerable attention to the universal meaning of *The Peasants* have failed to recognize how
Reymont's masterly creation of living characters makes it a work
of modern fiction instead of a poetic treatise on the countryside. United by a common heritage and acting as part of the
community, his characters are a true embodiment of both
poetry and national character and, therefore, they deserve close
study.

Traditionally, most critical attention goes to Boryna, who, with his eternal love for his land and sense of duty to it, is generally considered as the symbolic peasant. Indeed, the scene of his last sowing symbolizes the ultimate union of a peasant with his land, with Mother Earth. Boryna, after a prolonged illness, feels death approaching and rises from his bed. He goes out to sow the land, giving it first the sacred seed and finally his tired body. Written in sublime poetic language, that scene combines a realistic presentation of the old man's death with a symbolic vision of his union with the earth, to which he belongs forever.

To grasp the full significance of that climactic ending of the third part of the novel, we have to investigate Boryna's role in the two first parts. In *Spring* he is inactive; his existence casts a heavy shadow over the whole household, but he does not participate in the development of the family drama, since by the end of the second part, Boryna is practically eliminated from the plot when he is wounded during a fight in the woods, in another powerful scene which is the climax of that section.

Above all a man of action and violent passions, Maciej Boryna is introduced at the beginning of the novel in a series of scenes which stress these qualities. We encounter him first swearing and abusing everyone in the household because he has heard that a cow is dying. He kills the cow and afterward washes his hands at the well, associating the image of blood with him at his first appearance as a foreboding of the tragedy. Apparently, his main concern, though, is his farm. At first, his personal life is subordinated to improving it, acquiring more land, making crops grow. But in Boryna's nature there is also a strong indication of sexual passion: one of the first things we learn about him is his affair with Jewka, his former maid, who accuses the old man of making love to her and leaving her with a baby. Those two facets of his personality enter into his choice of his second wife. His initial interest in Jagna stems solely from her wealth, but soon he feels strong physical attraction for the young girl, who is famous for her beauty. The passion she awakens increases the image of blood associated with Boryna as he clashes violently with Antek after discovering the love affair between him and Jagna. The bloody fight results in Antek's expulsion from the family house soon to be occupied by the new mistress. The con-

flict between father and son worsens. Thus Boryna's passionate
character is fully revealed by the recurring image associated
with his land, his wife, and his son, making it psychologically and
artistically true.

The images of blood and violence which mark Boryna throughout the novel occur even at the reconciliation of father and
son. At the end of *Winter,* Antek, determined to resolve the conflict and having aimed his rifle at his father, changes his mind
and kills a forester who had wounded the old man instead. The
family ties prove stronger than hatred. Although this murder
leads to Antek's imprisonment, it buys Boryna's forgiveness. In
his last minute of consciousness he perceives in Antek his own
flesh and blood, and the same passions which have directed his
own life.

Another image which recurs throughout Reymont's entire
work is the destructive power of fire and finally, in *The Peasants,*
fire becomes fully symbolic. Earlier, in "Righteously," at the climax of the story, the purgative fire resolved all conflicts, bringing
purification not only to Jasiek but also to the village which had
turned against the fugitive. In *The Promised Land* the big factory
fire destroys Borowiecki's hopes and is a penalty for his desertion.
Reymont used the elemental power of fire both as a symbol of
justice and as an artistic device for solving complicated situations dramatically. He frequently symbolized the elemental
forces of nature, initially in self-explanatory, obvious associations, but gradually making their relationship to character and
plot development more sophisticated. In *The Comedienne,* Janka
Orlowska, attempting to escape the captivity of the big city,
found her first moment of spiritual consolation when she looked
into a river from the bank; here she met the mysterious stranger
who turned her thoughts toward eternity and brought her the
first foretaste of real happiness. Later, in *The Ferments,* think-
ing about the woods created a similar mood, and she experienced
a new wave of *élan vital* in the forest. In Reymont's works, these
natural symbols, sometimes used primitively, often underscore
the inner feelings of characters. At times they also emphasize the
climactic moments of the action, particularly in such scenes as

the first of a series of passionate encounters between Antek and Jagna in *The Peasants*.

In order to understand fully the role of these symbols we have to recall the development of the love story in that novel. After her marriage Jagna refused to meet her former suitor, but gradually Antek's persistence, the physical demands of her own young body, and the jealousy of the old man weakened her resistance. The increasing hostility between father and son, between Boryna as the representative of conservative and possessive forces and Antek as the embodiment of the power of youth and sexual attraction, reaches its height at a casual meeting at the inn. Antek asks Jagna to dance and catches her up in a wild whirl in front of the astounded crowd. Boryna's intervention results in a new fight. For Jagna, the dance revives old feelings, and in a few days she consents to a secret meeting with Antek. Blinded by their violent outburst of passion, the lovers do not notice Boryna. Boryna, resolving to erase the sin in his family, sets aflame the haystack in which they hide. Although they manage to escape, the purity of their natural love has been destroyed forever, burned out in the heat of the blaze. They will meet many more times, but they will never again experience the same overwhelming happiness.

The meaning of the symbolic use of fire is clear. A fire can be extinguished only by a more powerful fire; incest must result in the fire of hell. However, the early image of the upright Boryna as satanic, "running around the stack with the hayfork, looking like a devil in the bloody dawn," is disturbing. He is basically justified in defending his rights as a husband, but his attempt to erase the crime by committing a much graver one, the murder of his own son, is not. The suggestion that an evil power possesses Boryna is carried even further by the sheer contrast with Antek in the previously mentioned scene of the fight which climaxes *Winter*: when the old man intends to commit filicide, Antek saves him by killing the forester. Thus Antek's moral victory strengthens the association of Boryna with the devil in the previous scene.

However, symbolism in *The Peasants* should not be pushed too far, as some critics have done. At the turn of the century,

when the "Young Poland" movement based its literary criteria
on the poetics of Neo-Romanticism and its strong overtones of
Symbolism, which prevailed all over Europe at that time, a
symbolic interpretation of literary works led to subjective criticism which often obscured the work. Later, in the 1920's, when
psychological and psychoanalytical criticism began in Poland,
some critics applied the concepts of Freud and Jung to their
studies. One interesting interpretation of the symbols in *The
Peasants*, made by the Polish critic Jan N. Miller in 1926, found
that novel to be a modern version of universal myths and archetypes, associating Antek with Hercules and Jagna with Aphro-
dite, and so on, thus anticipating to some extent the concepts of
Claude Lévi-Strauss and other structuralists by almost half a
century.[14] Miller, incidentally, called Reymont "the poet of
community and type," although he claimed that the Nobel
Prize winner did "not have a fixed place in Polish literature,"
because he remained aloof from literary cliques and was in-
sufficiently recognized.

Basically, however, Reymont seems to have used symbols as
stylistic devices to underscore the psychology of his characters.
They are, above all, real people who live, love, hate, enjoy themselves and suffer with all-too-human intensity. They can be
interpreted as universal symbols but they are also endowed with
psychological validity. The novelist's primary goal in *The Peasants* was to depict as faithfully as possible the multiplicity of
village life, to create characters and conflicts which might have
existed under real conditions. When Reymont succeeded in charging his novel with universal meaning through the conscious
use of symbols, he enriched its structure without changing its
basic Realistic concept.

As the very breadth of the framework proves, his conception
of Realism was much broader and more ambitious than a purely
Naturalistic presentation of events and characters motivated by
biological forces would have been. One of the most striking
features of Reymont's conception of Realism is his creation of
characters, among whom Jagna may serve as the typical example.

Jagna embodies the psychology of a young woman spoiled
by her own beauty and the metaphysical notion of *das ewig*

Weibliche, "eternal womanhood." This concept was introduced into Polish literature by Przybyszewski, whose novels left a deep imprint on his contemporaries, particularly in Germany and Poland. Psychologically Jagna is like Izabella Lecka, the heroine in Prus's *The Doll,* who reveals a subconscious longing for sex which prevents her from accepting the protagonist Wokulski's love. But at the same time Jagna often appears to embody the "powers of mother nature," a quality which has prompted some critics to draw far-reaching conclusions about Reymont's use of myths and universal symbols. He probably intended, however, only to hint at the sexual drive directing her behavior and to construct a group of symbols to emphasize the psychological complexities of her sexuality. The conventional morality of the Victorian period and the resulting limits imposed upon nineteenth-century writers did not automatically disappear with the new century. In spite of his rather bold love scenes, Reymont did not want to lose his public by following Przybyszewski's school which professed the necessity of sexual freedom in art or, like Zeromski, to cause a deluge of public protest against his "immoral" novels. Instead, Reymont chose to veil the real nature of Jagna with symbols, to relate her to the "mother-earth," stressing her mysterious yearnings and presenting her as the personification of "eternal womanhood," a course many novelists chose over a more uninhibited presentation of human passions. Rita, the "woman of all time" in Conrad's *The Arrow of Gold,* is another such cryptic character. Reymont's characterization of Jagna is that of a Realist who is secure enough in his art to venture into myth and symbolism.

A close examination of the protagonist, Antek Boryna, seems to confirm a sober approach to Reymont's creative method. Having inherited all the passions and natural qualities for leadership of his father, Antek represents a new generation of peasants, by no means idealized. As his passion for Jagna gradually diminishes, Antek becomes more matter-of-fact, even pedestrian, in his concept of life. He continues his relationship with Jagna for a while, but after Boryna's death, when she becomes an easy prey for everyone and faces expulsion from the community, Antek must choose between protecting his former mistress and assuming his new position as an heir to his father's farm. He decides to abandon Jagna, concluding:

"Everything must go its own way. One has to plow in order to sow, one has to sow in order to harvest, and what is disturbing has to be weeded out, like a bad weed," a strict prehuman voice was talking inside him as if it were the voice of the land and the villages.[15]

His decision could be considered as morally wrong, even cowardice; however, it is justified psychologically and socially, for with old Boryna's death, Antek assumes his role as leader in the community. Once again Reymont proved here to be a Realist, remote from Romantic concepts which might have suggested a different ending. He knew the peasants sufficiently well not to be misled by the literary fashions of the past or even of his own age, which tended to idealize the peasants or to endow them with purely ideological motivations. Instead, he remained faithful to the truth as he saw it and turned it into an artistic vision.

III   Reymont's Lipce

Halfway between Warsaw and Lodz there is a railroad stop with the sign, "Lipce Reymontowskie." The adjective meaning "Reymont's" was added only in 1946, but the village of Lipce is several centuries old. It is located near another village, Krosnowa. Reymont had visited both villages when a literary career was only a distant dream. Years later, he chose Lipce as the setting for The Peasants.

Naturally, the problem of separating the actual village from the fictive one in his depiction of Lipce has occupied many critics,[16] who hoped to throw new light on Reymont's technique. However, in spite of more or less detailed examination of the village, its history, inhabitants, and folklore, such attempts have proved futile. Rzeuska, after discussing the difference between reality and fiction in general, concludes that it is "not the place of action in the exact meaning of those words that matters but a universal presentation of the whole milieu of the peasants' life."[17] The universal associations with a given place, then, play the decisive role in the novel, no matter how closely the fictional Lipce corresponds in detail to the factual setting, since it is those universal qualities that transform reality into art and make it comprehensible in terms of literature. It is one of the basic features of *The Peasants*, that characters are presented as individuals, and the setting achieves a higher, more general role, serving as the background for the action.

Reymont depicted his Lipce with all the folklore linguistic details particular to that specific village; by making it individual, he succeeded in making it typical, a goal achieved only by a few masters of fiction. The symbolic images further enhanced the setting, charging it with universal meaning far beyond the actual village of Lipce, beyond any local or even national boundaries. Even so, *The Peasants* contains almost documentary details which make the novel a contribution to the history of the cultural and social development of Poland, as Balzac's and Zola's works contribute to the social history of France. Many of these details are of Lipce.

At first glance the choice of village seems dictated purely by the novelist's personal experience there; however, a closer look reveals its appropriateness as the setting for an epic novel of the Polish countryside. Deep in rural Poland, remote from modern life, and almost self-sufficient economically, Lipce preserved the patriarchal social structure, ancient customs, religious rituals, and family structure with all the inherent conflicts existing within the families and in the community. This way of life was encountered outside of Poland, too, since a similar social structure prevailed in many countries dependent on an agricultural economy. A comparison between Lipce and Rognes in Zola's *La Terre* reveals such striking similarities that many critics have hastened to draw conclusions about the influence of the French novel on *The Peasants*. That this influence does not go beyond certain similarities and common trends has been proved in a brilliant essay by Franck Louis Schoell, who concludes "At first glance what a deep, impassable gulf separates *The Peasants* from *La Terre!*"[18] Nonetheless, the novels have much in common, not only in subject matter and setting, but also and especially in the elevation of simple human experiences to a universal dimension. Reymont's novel comes as close to the truth of the human condition as a work of literature can. It is a novel of rare complexity, an expression of spirit which goes beyond national boundaries, but which remains unmistakably Polish.

Lipce itself reflects the complexity in the novel. The community is deeply involved in the drama slowly unfolding at the Borynas, but at the same time it goes its own way in accordance with the old customs, following the pace set by nature, the coming and passing of seasons which bring work and relaxation, joys and sorrows, busy days and refreshing nights. The Borynas' house occupies the central place in the village exactly as it does in the novel, and there is an uninterrupted, mutual relationship between the community and each of the four central characters who live there. The events affecting the Borynas affect Lipce to almost an equal extent, at least in the first half of the novel. In the remaining two parts the tensions in that family ease and are replaced by new conflicts which involve a larger number of characters and sometimes the whole community, such as the struggles of the village with the German colonists, or with the Russian authorities over the public school. Both issues are violently opposed by the residents of Lipce, who want neither foreign neighbors nor a foreign school because of their patriotism, deep devotion to tradition, and desire for an unchanged pattern of life.

Two characters in the novel primarily responsible for maintaining contact between the Borynas and the village are an old beggar woman, Jagustynka, and Rocho, the travelling emissary of the national movement, a movement never precisely identified. While the tragic frustrated Jagustynka functions as the local gossip, stirring up new conflicts and aggravating them with her sharp tongue, Rocho, who serves mostly as a peacemaker, borders on the sacrosanct; Rocho's mission is to uplift human hearts with the gospel, patriotic as well as religious. By moving those two characters from one household to another, the author connects various subplots, introduces new inhabi-

tants, and creates an opportunity to introduce the events, customs, and religious services in Lipce.

This method of advancing the action through the movement
of characters is followed from the very first pages of the novel,
in which the priest strikes up a conversation with several women
whose gossip gives some meaningful clues to the plot. The gossip
also serves another artistic purpose: presented through the eyes
of a character, description becomes an integral part of the plot.
The balance between description and movement of the plot is
successfully maintained in the first half of the work, but, later,
the two tend to be staggered. The lack of balance has a further
implication for Reymont's style.

The relationship between the main characters and the community, on the one hand, and the balance between action and
description on the other, structure the novel. An analysis of the
relationship between these two factors explains many facets of
Reymont's art. The main plot, the incest in the Boryna family,
concerns the community, too; eventually, Jagna is violently
expelled by the villagers. Her personal drama becomes a core
of the action which unites all the characters and the community
as a whole in the climax of the novel. The subplots have previously been resolved, their climaxes placed strategically at the
end of each volume. Such a climax occurs, for example, at the
end of *Winter* when the villagers, hitherto separate and socially
stratified, learn that the forest which traditionally belongs to
Lipce has been sold by the squire, they unite there and fight
for their rights. The battle, described in the best tradition of
Sienkiewicz's historical novels, results in a victory attained at a
heavy cost. Boryna is fatally wounded, and he is subsequently
replaced by Antek, who will become the leader of the community. In the next volumes of the novel, when the Russian
authorities press for a new school with instruction in Russian,
Antek, released from jail, where he had been kept for killing
the forester, organizes a boycott against the vote for the new
school. He and his former rival for Jagna's favors, Mateusz,
represent the new spirit of the united peasants, the young
generation leading their class toward a new, more enlightened
way of life.

Throughout the novel scattered scenes contain exact, almost documentary descriptions of religious holidays, observances, and rituals. United by the same faith, the peasants find in the church not only spiritual guidance but also the strength and splendor they need to endure their hard work. They go to church to celebrate the holidays, to worship, and to indulge in mystical experiences incomprehensible to their simple minds but deeply rooted in their souls. Sometimes they also find there good advice in purely practical matters. The priest publicly condemns Antek for his immoral relationship with Jagna, but at the same time he works hard to reconcile the Borynas in their family quarrel.

Presented realistically and, at times, satirically, the priest is the village's highest authority, but Rocho is the real spiritual leader of the community. A mysterious, evangelical emissary of the underground patriotic movement, Rocho is at first only a wanderer spending his old age travelling from one village to another. Gradually, he discloses his true mission, but the full extent of it is revealed only at the end of the novel when we learn of his clandestine distribution of propaganda in Lipce against the Russians.

Actually Rocho is the only major character who links the novel with politics, thus placing it in a definite historical context. Incidental remarks about Boryna's participating in an uprising and a barely outlined story of comradeship in arms between Boryna's servant, Kuba, and the squire's brother, Jacek, contribute little to dating the exact time of the action. The events in *The Peasants*, subtitled in its first editions "A Contemporary Novel," could have taken place in the early twentieth century almost as well as some fifty years earlier, in spite of the definite historical, political, and even social differences between the two periods, differences which grew out of the Polish national uprisings in 1830 and 1863. Obviously, the author's intention was to avoid political implications and to create a truly universal picture of a Polish village, patriarchal and centuries old, unrelated to any particular historical period. Such avoidance of milieu is quite uncommon in Polish literature, especially that of the nineteenth century, for Polish literature has been tra-

ditionally concerned with Poland's history and with political and
social issues. Reymont placed his novel somewhat outside the
main stream of Polish fiction and led to criticism of his method.[19]

IV   *One of Them*

A short study devoted to Reymont and his art, written by
Franck Louis Schoell in 1918, "Les Paysans polonais vus par
un des leurs" (The Polish Peasants as Seen by One of Them)[20]
describes not only the novelist's origins and his profound knowledge of the social milieu presented in the novel, but also attrib-
utes a special meaning to the technique and style of his work.
Schoell points out the relationship between the novelist's knowledge of the subject matter and the method of presentation in
the novel. In order to understand Reymont's style in *The Peasants*, we have to explain it in historical context of contemporary
developments in European literatures in general.

By the end of the nineteenth century the role of an author in
relation to his topic seemed to be a foregone conclusion. The
masters of Realism, particularly the "new school" of Flaubert
in France, Turgenev and Tolstoy in Russia, Henry James and
William Dean Howells in America, to name a few, had firmly
established that there was no room for the "lyrical I," a first-
person narrative from the point of view of the omniscient author.
The story was supposed "to tell itself," the author to disappear
from the scene and to let his characters act by themselves.[21]
Howells, the American champion of Realism, had this to say
about Turgenev's art:

His fiction is to the last degree dramatic. The persons are sparely
described, and briefly accounted for, and they are left to transact
their affairs, whatever they are, with the least possible comment
or explanation from the author. The effect flows naturally from
their characters, and when they have done or said a thing you
conjecture why as unerringly as you would if they were people
whom you knew outside of a book.[22]

This method changed by the turn of the century. Because of
the new, more subjective approach of the Symbolist school, the
role of the author became more personal and obvious, although

the followers of the Realistic method still to a large extent upheld the principle of objectivity. The author was supposed not only to make his characters speak their own tongue but also to render the description in the same style. The problem of unifying artistically these two factors occupied the authors and scholars in their theoretical studies for a long time. In his own work, Reymont solved it by identifying the author with the subjects of his novel. A Polish scholar, Stefania Skwarczynska, cites *The Peasants* as an example of such identification, in which description is written partly in dialect because that is the characters' form of speech.[23]

It has often been emphazized that *The Peasants* has two distinct styles; the style for the narrator's voice, and that for the characters in the dialogues. This stylistic distinction, however, works in the novel in one way only: while the characters never use "literary" language and speak only dialect, the narrator's voice is more flexible. His "literary" poetic and highly expressive language is often permeated with elements of folklore speech; especially by the end of the novel the narration is rendered almost entirely in dialect, which becomes a new poetic language as well.

Dialect used as the narrator's voice was part of the new poetics introduced by the writers of "Young Poland," who are often referred to as Neo-Romantics or Modernists. Wyspianski, Tetmajer, Kasprowicz and scores of other contemporary writers brought to Polish literature the treasures of Polish dialects, using them as stylistic devices to enrich and refresh the language. Novels and stories written entirely in dialect such as Tetmajer's *Tales of the Tatras* or plays like Wyspianski's *The Wedding* (1901) marked the change and achieved great success for their style.

Reymont, who reacted sensitively to contemporary trends in literature, understood the importance of the new method. As we have seen, some of his early stories already used narration in dialect, too, but only in *The Peasants* did he elevate such a technique to primary significance, and achieved highly artistic effects. Nature, whether described in the landscape, the fury of the elements, or the beauty of the forests, appeared in a new light as if presented by a master who knew how to combine the natural poetry of dialect with the best of the literary tradition. The author, through his style, could identify himself both with his characters and with the spirit of his land and his nation, becoming, indeed, "one of them" in every word and phrase.

His technique involved, however, a danger Reymont could not avoid. Descriptive passages lose the sense of immediacy of the characters and their environment. Apparently this was the price he had to pay; the poetics of his age were so intensely charged with symbolism that works often departed from reality into regions of metaphysical experience. As a result, Reymont's descriptive style, especially in the later parts of the novel, becomes heavy, overloaded with artificial images and vocabulary, sometimes full of superfluous metaphors. At first, compact and unified, the novel breaks by the end of *Winter* and becomes torn between the realistic action and symbolic descriptions.

Reymont had always been susceptible to literary influences, a danger to his art because he lacked a firm esthetic philosophy. Even in his mature period he often succumbed to the influence of contemporary trends and individual writers, and he often lost his own style in his attempts to imitate or to adapt the motifs and methods of others. As a result, his writing toward the end of *The Peasants* and his later work show a peculiar mixture of Realism and Symbolism, of following tradition and searching for new idioms. Sometimes this mixture resulted in meaningless clichés, in scientific concepts of the Naturalistic school combined with the traditional pathos of battle pieces, as if Zola and Sienkiewicz stood side by side as literary models. Curiously enough, Reymont displayed the same confusion in his political views. He allied himself with the right-wing National Democratic Party of Dmowski, for instance, but for a while was also interested in Socialism as a new progressive force. His lack of philosophical backbone impoverished his late work, depriving it of the unity of impact of *The Peasants*. Therefore, that novel, which captures the universal meaning of human existence through its study of the lives of simple people, remains Reymont's highest achievement. As the American critic Rupert Hughes said in appraising Reymont's role in world literature,

. . . we are all peasants in a sense and the peasants must uphold us. Anything that makes for their happiness or their misery creeps upward through the whole social structure. Reymont's *Peasants* are, therefore, all of us. His theme is fundamental and, therefore, enormous. It is as important to all nations as to any one nation. The novel itself is a universal work in a sense beyond almost any other.[24]

CHAPTER 7

A Historical Trilogy

THE PEASANTS was an enormous success. It put Reymont in the front ranks of Polish literature at a time when it was mostly dominated by poetry, won him international fame, and eventually a Nobel Prize. A German translation in 1912 made *The Peasants* familiar to Western Europe and began to establish Reymont's reputation outside of Poland.

Although he was exhausted from working on the long novel, Reymont was determined to continue writing even at the expense of his health. He felt that the responsibility for maintaining the high standard of Polish literature rested almost entirely upon him and Zeromski, who were the two most important novelists since the old generation of writers had ceased to dominate Polish letters by the turn of the century. The older writers concurred with Reymont's view of his position. Eliza Orzeszkowa, who had been one of the leading exponents of Realism, wrote Reymont after the publication of *The Peasants* that "As the globe rests on Atlas' shoulders, so Polish fiction rests on you."[1]

It must have been a heavy burden. In the second half of the nineteenth century Polish writers such as Sienkiewicz, Prus, and Orzeszkowa had achieved an artistic level in fiction that compared with the best in the world literature. At the beginning of the new century new writers, like Zeromski and Przybyszewski, captured public attention with their novels and short stories embodying a new esthetic.

Because the writer had a special role in Polish national life, because he was expected to achieve more than artistry, the public's response to him was especially important. After the Revolution of 1905, which brought new hope for the country's

94

independence, the "Young Poland" literary movement, Neo-Romanticism, not only revived the artistic aims of Romanticism, but reemphasized those national and patriotic issues which had motivated to a great extent the Polish Romantic movement of the 1830's. "Young Poland" in this respect differed from similar movements in other European countries by departing from its decadent beginnings and the "art for art's sake" slogans and steered toward national goals, particularly at the end of the 1910's.

Wilhelm Feldman, the leading Polish critic of that period, expressed the demands and concerns of the public when in 1902 he wrote comparing Polish Romantic poets with the Neo-Romantic movement of "Young Poland":

The content of their songs embraced the living truths about the freedom of nations and individuals, about the justice which should reign among the nations, about the religion of spirit molding the matter and defying the reign of force.... These are the Polish truths, born independently from other nations.... Young Poland has revived these and understood them more critically, more contemporarily; she recalled them and strengthened the basic cultural facts of life and eternity.[2]

Reymont, who never associated himself very closely with "Young Poland," was nevertheless aware both of the basic issues and of public opinion. Spending most of his time abroad, he remained in touch with the Polish press and the major figures of Polish intellectual life, who lived both in Poland and Western Europe, especially France. There was hardly an important Polish writer or artist who did not spend some period in the capital of the world, as Paris was generally considered. And Reymont divided his time between creative writing and his Polish friends.

Still another factor must have influenced the author of *The Peasants* to change his focus from contemporary topics to history. Historical romance was immensely popular in Poland. Beginning with the inexhaustible Jozef Ignacy Kraszewski, who wrote more than two hundred novels, up to Henryk Sienkiewicz, whose historical trilogy and *The Teutonic Knights* and *Quo Vadis?* won him literary fame in Poland and abroad, the historical romance enjoyed the widest acclaim among Polish readers. Seemingly, a successful historical novel published in Poland granted fame, popularity, and a secure place in the Pantheon of the nation, a fact which the success of Zeromski's *The Ashes* (1904) seemed to prove once more. Its publication coincided with the general revival of Neo-Romantic patriotic trends and was, as Henryk Markiewicz recently remarked, "the nearest, the most expressive historical metaphor for striving toward independence, which at the turn of the century again gained more strength among the basic strata of the nation."[3] Reymont must have felt it his patriotic obligation to contribute a historical novel to the theme of the national struggle for independence.

The idea of writing a historical novel first occurred to Reymon as early as 1908, before he had finished the last volume of his tetralogy. At first he considered a trilogy dealing with the major military upheavals in Poland's fight for independence in the nineteenth century: 1812—the Napoleonic campaign and the role of the Polish forces fighting in it; 1830—the November uprising against the Russians; 1863—the January uprising, which had become the major theme in Zeromski's short stories and early novels.[4] Soon, however, apparently attracted by the peasant character of the Kosciuszko Insurrection against the Russians in 1794, Reymont must have decided to make it the topic of a novel describing the 1793 partition of Poland between Russia, Prussia, and Austria. Originally he intended to focus on the leader of the Insurrection, Thaddeus Kosciuszko, and the spontaneous support he received from the masses, particularly the peasants to whom he promised freedom and social justice; his program was somewhat modeled on the democratic principles he had been able to observe during his service in the Revolutionary War in the United States. The novel, however, took another direction and the historical account of Kosciuszko served only as one of the motifs. The trilogy entitled *The Year 1794* was published in consecutive volumes as *The Last Diet of the Republic* (1911), *Nil Desperandum* (1916), and *Insurrection* (1918). Reymont also planned a fourth volume devoted to Dabrowski's Legion and the beginning of the Napoleonic era, but the publisher thought it untimely in 1917 when Poland's independence was almost granted and interest centered on contemporary events. The author abandoned it, as he wrote, "with considerable regret."[5]

His regret is understandable. The novel involved him emotionally; he had found a new subject for his epic talent. Always attracted by large panoramic scenes with masses of people moving in sweeping waves, aroused by elemental human emotions, colorful and exciting in their constant changes, Reymont had not written with such scope and breadth since *The Promised Land*. After the microcosm of Lipce, the new project presented breathtaking possibilities for exploring the whole of national life in a dramatic, desperate struggle against overpowering enemies, on various levels and in a multitude of perspectives. Reymont's attitude toward this work is well described in Adam Szelagowski's obituary of Reymont, published in 1926:

The Year 1794, a historical novel, was his most favorite work which, perhaps because it had been neglected and forgotten, he loved more than *The Peasants*, and, as he himself confessed as late as last Spring, he considered his life's major achievement.[6]

Unfortunately, neither the critics nor the reading public shared the author's opinion. Most readers considered the novel an artistic failure, much below the standards of both *The Peasants* and the best Polish historical fiction. Because, moreover, it appeared on the eve of and during World War I, when the public was concerned with the immediate issue of regaining the country's independence, it could not have the popular appeal of similar novels published earlier in the nineteenth century. Today it can be judged more objectively.

I *The Last Diet*

The historical novel in its modern form, patterned on the works of Sir Walter Scott, was enormously popular in Poland because its Romanticism corresponded to the mood of mid-nineteenth century Poland and because it nostalgically appealed to the pride in the past glories of this once powerful nation, now ineffectual and divided among foreign powers. The historical novel thus not only reflected the nation's history, but also served as a vehicle to articulate those hopes and dreams which otherwise had to remain silenced. Jozef Ignacy Kraszewski, who labored long to give the captive nation an impressive cycle of novels which recaptured Poland's past from the earliest times to the end of the eighteenth century, laid solid foundations for the further development of the historical novel in Polish letters.

In the second half of the nineteenth century a new and bright talent achieved national fame: Henryk Sienkiewicz's *With Fire and Sword* (1883), a historical novel about the Polish-Cossack war in the seventeenth century became a widely acclaimed best seller. By combining a solid historical background with an adventure romance partly modeled after Alexandre Dumas's novels, Sienkiewicz introduced the new form into Polish historical fiction. The remaining parts of the trilogy, *The Deluge* and *Pan Michael,* and his late novel *The Teutonic Knights,* continued to lead that genre, and they remain best sellers in Poland even today. While *Quo Vadis?* accounts for Sienkiewicz's international reputation and his being awarded the Nobel Prize for literature in 1905, it is the historical trilogy which still captures the imagination of Polish readers.

Sienkiewicz's success, achieved while most writers were concerned with contemporary issues, was an unusual phenomenon. But in the years immediately preceding the outbreak of World War I, as the question of national independence grew more acute under shifting political and social conditions, novelists and historians turned to Poland's past. Tales of adventure, national epics, and scholarly historical studies all reflected the growing nationalistic fervor for political independence. By the end of the first decade of the century, the question of national independence had become the dominant consideration of intellectuals. Naturally, Reymont was deeply involved in these questions, and they must have influenced his historical novel.

It has been pointed out often that the background of Reymont's trilogy *The Year 1794* was firmly based on historical studies, numerous memoirs, newspapers, and even fragments of historical novels,[7] but critics have failed to explain why Reymont changed his original intention and set his novel in 1794 instead of 1812. The explanation, however, seems to be simple. After the success of his great novel Reymont was generally considered as "the bard of the Polish peasants' soul." When his interests turned to the historical novel, he chose the most plebeian of Polish national heroes, Kosciuszko, and his Insurrection. In order to emphasize the democratic elements in the national upheaval, he exposed the corruption and treason of the aristocrats who ruled the country. Reymont thus created a striking contrast between the peasants and aristocrats—social groups which diametrically opposed each other on almost every major issue. By creating this contrast he challenged traditional historiography, which emphasized the leading role of the nobility, not without severe criticism, to be sure, and which neglected the role of the peasants as the decisive element in the national struggle for independence. Reymont had already introduced his view of Polish history in *The Peasants* by symbolizing the spirit of national solidarity in the person of the peasant-loving landowner, Jacek, who felt closer to his former comrade-in-arms, Kuba, than to his own brother. Reymont went even further in the final scenes of the historical trilogy. He believed that the peasants played a decisive role in the life of the country, and his novels were among the very few in Polish literature to reflect that belief. The protagonists in the works of Sienkiewicz and Zeromski had been mainly noblemen, and peasants appeared only incidentally, but Reymont emphasized the peasants in the historical process. Unfortunately, he succeeded only in part. While many scenes in *The Year 1794* deal with the peasants as a new social force, the protagonist, Sewer Zareba, in spite of his Jacobin and revolutionary connections, is another nobleman hero of Polish literature. He is much more progressive than his predecessors, but his characterization is still a compromise between Reymont's own convictions and the powerful pressure of tradition. The choice of that particular period in Poland's history is still, however, in full accord with the author's concept of the historical role of the peasants in the past, and his hopes for the approaching future.

The structure of *The Last Diet* and the other works in the

trilogy is very close to that of *The Promised Land*. Made up of a variety of characters, places, scenes, and events, it is linked together by the protagonist who, like Borowiecki in the earlier novel, moves from one environment to another, permitting the author to enter different milieux and to tie them into one plot. As in the other novel, the love story, Zareba's unhappy affair with Iza, is an attempt to introduce romance, but it does not play an important role in the intrinsic structure of the novel. The love plot soon becomes a nuisance, since the real interest focuses on a patriotic conspiracy involving Zareba. Accordingly, the novel focuses on historical events, in particular on the last days of the country's independence and its last diet.

The last Polish Diet, which assembled in Grodno in June 1793, makes a dramatic and tragic story by itself. Under extreme Russian pressure, the last King of Poland, Stanislaw August Poniatowski, and the great majority of the Diet become helpless tools in the skillful hands of the Russian envoy Jacob Sievers. Although he superficially attempted to convince public opinion in Europe that the Poles could exercise their free will to vote for an alliance with Russia, as it was officially phrased, he grew more and more arrogant, until a final open intervention by the Russian army forced the Diet to accept the occupants' terms. In spite of the general cynical attitude toward the politics of the Polish aristocrats, who cared more for personal favors and material gains than for the Republic, a small group of courageous patriots defended the national cause and resisted the enforced vote to the end. Powerless against the big empire of Catherine II, supported only by public opinion, they fought openly and clandestinely and were ready to call for nationwide revolution in the event of a Russian victory. Their determination and passionate resistance illuminated the most glorious pages in Poland's history, and may still serve today as an example of bravery and devotion in defending a nation's independence to the very last. The striking similarity between the events of 1793 and recent history gives Reymont's novel renewed meaning after fifty years.

The first part of Reymont's trilogy, *The Last Diet*, encompasses one month of that dramatic struggle, August 1 to September 2, 1793. The novel is set almost exclusively in Grodno, with a few short scenes outside the town. It opens with a feast given in Sievers's honor by Polish aristocrats, each of whom is trying to exceed the other in servility and adulation. Among the characters, who are in the main drawn from real political and social figures, appears the fictitious Zareba, who comes to the party as a stranger. With the introduction of a stranger, Reymont has ample opportunity to show to the protagonist an impressive gallery of politicians, diplomats, careerists, and social-ites, including Zareba's former fiancée, Iza. He also meets his fellow-conspirators and reveals the real reason for his coming to Grodno: he is on a mission of the revolutionary committee of Polish patriots. Using a time-honored device of blending fiction with reality, Reymont presents a conversation between Zareba and General Jakub Jasinski, a leader in the revolution-ary movement. However well known since ancient times, such a device makes Zareba more convincing because he is con-stantly acting among historical persons, and also dramatizes history by presenting it in the adventures of a fictional charac-ter not bound to the biography of a real person.

This device, often used in nineteenth-century fiction, allows the author to present actual events and at the same time make them alive to the reader. When Sienkiewicz's *With Fire and Sword* was serialized, for instance, people prayed for the sal-vation of its protagonist, Skrzetuski, as if the success of his mission could have turned back history and changed its tragic course. Fiction, well written, convincing, and emotionally involv-ing, performs its special psychological and social function in difficult times, particularly in periods of national disaster and the dark years of foreign yoke. However, whereas Sienkiewicz concentrated on presenting the adventures of his protagonists against a traditionally accepted interpretation of historical events, Reymont focused on the social causes of Poland's fall, and exposed the political machinery behind the scenes. The plots introduced in the first chapter of the novel—the political situa-tion, the conspiracy, the love story—contribute to an overall picture of parties and factions in their struggle at the Diet; numerous subplots, loosely connected to the protagonist, play supporting roles and explore through Zareba's adventures various causes and aspects of the main theme. A great many of these incidental subplots and characters disappear in the course of the novel. The reader familiar with Polish history would certainly expect Jasinski, for instance, to play a major role. Instead, the jovial fictitious Kaczanowski, very much like the unforgettable Polish Falstaff, Zagloba, from Sienkiewicz's trilogy, occupies more and more space. Thus the structure of *The Last Diet* is uneven; many themes are dropped before they have been fully developed, many characters appear without contributing either to the progress of action or in their relationship to the plot. In general, the novel lacks a structural unity, and this made it inferior in comparison with other novels in Polish historical fiction. Nonetheless, *The Last Diet* contains some chapters of high artistic value.

The opening chapter deserves attention because of the mood it evokes. Beside fulfilling the usual expository function, it renders the general tone of regret, sadness, and despair which reigned in the soon-to-perish nation. It sounds like a sad refrain in the famous scene of the grand polonaise danced at the party with its recurring symbolic image of a Polish noblewoman dancing with the Russian envoy. Against the memories of Poland's greatness and victories which the melody recalls, resounds the momentous staccato: "And Mr. Sievers was leading the ball with Madame Ozarowska."[8]

Such impressive images render the atmosphere of doom awaiting Poland. And although even the bravest endeavors of the patriots could not have averted the course of history, we follow their desperate struggle with the intense feeling that it was not in vain. Reymont's novel, then, fulfills its social and psychological functions in awakening feelings of compassion for the Polish patriots. And that was precisely the author's goal.

Reymont knew how to evoke these feelings by strongly contrasting the small group of devoted patriots with the large majority of nobility, who are either corrupt or indifferently cynical. As often happens in fiction, the villains are masterly vivid three-dimensional portrayals while the representatives of the right cause are rather colorless with the possible exception

of Zareba, who is vigorous, energetic, and adventuresome but
not always convincing in his superhuman virtues. Besides the
historical figures, Reymont introduces hundreds of incidental
fictional characters to create mass scenes in the pattern explored
earlier in *The Promised Land*. The technique he invented there,
involving the constant movement of large crowds of people,
frequent change of scene, and minute presentation of even
unimportant characters through dialogues and action, finds an
even more colorful and picturesque dimension in *The Last
Diet*. Here, too, his linguistic ability is even more notable.
While in his industrial novel Reymont captured various
peculiarities of speech of the Polish, German, and Jewish characters, here he recreates the whole idiom of the language at the
end of the eighteenth century, a language made up of a special
mixture of Polish, French, and Latin. He also frequently uses
obsolete expressions and vocabulary in dialogues as well as
in descriptions, often to achieve the unity of style he had in
The Peasants.

The crowd of petty gentry in the streets of Grodno not only
dresses, moves, and acts but also speaks differently from the
aristocrats occupying their luxurious residences, and from the
plebeian soldiers whom Zareba secretly mobilizes in the forests. Those two social groups, the gentry and the peasants,
introduce into the novel a new social force which is given a
more detailed treatment later, especially in the third volume
of the trilogy. The gentry of Grodno give the novel local color,
yet *The Last Diet* focuses on the court and the aristocracy,
whose role decided the outcome of the political struggle. Zareba, moving freely among the three social groups, links them
together and creates action which is often suspended for the
sake of historical detail, and which digresses into the adventures of his secret mission.

Although there is an obvious link between the techniques
of the novel and *The Promised Land*, there is little evidence
of a close link between *The Last Diet* and *The Peasants*. The
peasants appear only incidentally; their entrance is postponed
to the second volume. Characters such as Kacper, Zareba's
orderly and friend, are merely sketched with some indication

of their revolutionary ideas and hopes for equal social rights. There is, however, a major difference between the two novels on the issue of Poland's independence. In *The Peasants* the Russians were practically absent; when they appeared they either were referred to as "watchmen," or played a minor role in incidental issues such as the Russification of the school. Here "the allies," as Reymont constantly calls them with ironic delight, occupy a prominent place and are represented by political actions as well as by a series of characters such as the cunning Sievers, the brutal Tsytsyanov, and the ruthless Zubov. This change in Reymont's attitude toward politics and the issues of nationalism is attributed by most critics to the author's growing involvement with the National Democrats and their increasing role in the Russian Duma which resulted in more open demands for Poland's autonomy in the Russian Empire, and, after the Revolution of 1905, more freedom of expression. The novelist faced the dilemma of choosing between his apolitical attitude and a personal involvement in the rapidly growing problems of partisan politics. Roman Dmowski, the leader of the National Democracy, spared no efforts to conscript Reymont to his camp and, indeed, the novelist found himself in an awkward situation.

At first basically indifferent to the political struggle between the Socialists and National Democrats gaining momentum in the first years of the century, he began to lean toward the latter, although maintaining his independent position as a writer. By the time he was finishing *The Peasants* the ideology of the National Democratic camp seemed to overshadow his interest in social issues and resulted in scenes of social solidarity in the community in its last volume as well as in short stories hostile to Socialism. A warm welcome from the National Democrats and various forms of encouragement on the part of some editors served to strengthen these political views. When, however, he began to write his historical trilogy he faced still another difficult dilemma.

The end of the eighteenth century was marked by the most revolutionary upheaval and social clashes in Poland's history. The political opposition in 1793 was modeled in many respects after the Jacobins during the French Revolution. The radical leaders, Hugo Kollataj and his circle, formed the left wing of the opposition, while the more moderate politicians sought a milder solution, trying to avoid bloodshed among the compatriots. Reymont, who was determined to write a novel faithful to historical facts, had to choose between emphasizing the social issues and the revolutionary character of their solution, or merely patriotic struggle for national independence. Either could have serious political implications for his own career, for a historical novel was still regarded in Poland as the political manifesto of its author. Reymont tried, then, to keep his novel from becoming an ideological weapon in his own days and to preserve his artistic independence in an impartial objective presentation of history.

It was most probably the political objectivity of *The Year 1794* which caused its cool reception in Poland. In most cases representative of the official lines of their political parties, the critics could not be satisfied with its general tone and ideological non-commitment. Even in recent times, the Marxists have attacked the novel vehemently for lack of political involvement. But what seems more important is the fact that apart from the presence or absence of strong ideological coloring the novel suffers artistically from the lack of a unifying philosophy of history—a lack which always seriously affected Reymont's works. Perhaps the critics who require a major author to take a definite point of view have a case. Especially in Poland, where one was constantly exposed to political fluctuation, with external dangers threatening its very existence, philosophical commitment all too often meant political affiliation. There artistic objectivity seemed to be a luxury a major artist could not afford.

Zareba, the protagonist, is deeply involved in revolutionary activities. We learn early in the novel that he had been to France; when, after his return, he encountered the King of Poland for the first time, he muttered: "I have seen a king's head falling down under the guillotine, and the executioner grabbed it by the hair and showed it to the people." However, Zareba wants to fight the Russians more than anything else, since national independence is for him equally as important as civil rights. How can he then fight for his country, which is ruled by a legitimate king, and against the king at the same time? That internal conflict reaches a climax in the third part of the trilogy, when Reymont presents two camps, the revolutionaries and the legitimists, in a fierce confrontation during the Insurrection, and makes Zareba choose between his beliefs and his duty. In *The Last Diet* these motifs are merely hinted at because the author tried to remain objective and to concentrate on presenting the whole complex situation during the last days of the country which was doomed to disappear for the next hundred and fifty years.

Even with his attempt to remain uncommitted, Reymont makes the reader sharply aware of the social injustice in the lot of the peasants. In the forest when Zareba meets the volunteers who had escaped from the Russian army and are gathering to join the remnants of the Polish forces, they recite a somber litany of complaints, a litany resembling the famous passages in Zeromski's novels and plays:

"And who will take care of those whom the enemy captured? Who will help these poor orphans?" rose a gloomy voice. "So many of them creep under the sticks, and even a dog will not whine for them."

"About those thousands escaping from the enemy, who will care?"

"As a swarm of bees without a queen we spread to perish in vain."

"And if someone escapes the pursuit he won't escape death from starvation, he won't indeed."

"They have sold us," moaned someone in a drawling voice like an echo reflected a hundred times.

"By force, by using power they drafted us into the army, they grew fat on our poverty, they paved half of the world with our bones, and at the end they sold us to the enemy."

"They sold the whole motherland," as an echo moaned the same voice again.

"Nobody went to the enemy voluntarily, perhaps the officers only, and so when there was a chance everyone ran away as if to his own mother."

"And your mother, soldier, is death itself, your fortune wounds alone, your rest a grave. Every lord's mansion stands on the foundation of your bones, soldier, every field has been saturated with your sweat, and you, peasant, even if you worked your arms down to the stub, if you won a hundred battles, and faithfully gave the last drop of your blood for your country, you would always be a slave. There is no land for you, no heaven, no shelter, not even a doghouse where you could rest your poor head. You are the last before God and before people, the last one."[9]

This lengthy quotation permits a glimpse not only of the author's attitude toward social injustice but also of his changing style. Many similar passages imitate the peasants' solemn speech, with poetic repetitions and chantlike rhythm of recurring phrases. The pages devoted to the misery of the peasants who had served in the Polish army and were deceived by the corrupted aristocrats are among the best in the novel. Permeated with deep human compassion, they achieve an astonishing artistic perfection.

The world of the aristocracy and the petty gentry is painted in different colors; Reymont does not hide his contempt for their general moral decay reigning at that time. In one scene an old gentleman makes a bet that he can drink a barrel of wine with one breath and wins, to everyone's amusement. Similar scenes of drinking, eating, playing cards and quarreling make the novel a document of customs, morals, faithfully rendering the atmosphere of the epoch. These vignettes are submerged, however, in the prevailing somber tone in a mood of the oncoming doom which reaches its climax in the last chapters, which depict the hopeless fight in the Diet assembled under the point of Russian guns. In a perfect accord between the historical climax and the structural climax, *The Last Diet* ends with the Diet voting for the second partition of Poland.

II Nil Desperandum

The variety of complex subplots introduced in the first volume of the trilogy broadens in the second one entitled *Nil Desperandum* (Never Despair). In spite of the lamentable conditions in Poland after the second partition in 1793, the conspirators did not, indeed, fall into despair. Through their sacrifices and patriotic endeavors, a Polish army was formed again both in the northern and in the southern provinces, and a leader arose whose name and authority were impressive enough to unite quarreling political factions. He was Thaddeus Kosciuszko, a hero of the American Revolutionary War and the most able and courageous general of the Polish campaign of 1792.

Born into a family of the country gentry, Kosciuszko graduated from the cadet school in Warsaw; having received a King's fellowship, he went to Paris and became a military engineer. Soon after returning to Poland, he left the country in 1775 for personal reasons and joined the Revolutionary Army in America where he gradually worked his way up to the rank of Brigadier General under George Washington. After his second return to Poland, in 1784, he fought victoriously against the Russians in many battles and then retired without associating himself with any political group. He was obviously an ideal commander-in-chief for the uprising laboriously prepared by the conspirators; his deeply democratic ideas and patriotic spirit secured the support of the masses, a support which was badly needed for the survival of the country. He was, as the Polish historian Oscar Halecki remarked, a man with "the high merit of having, for the first time, interested all classes of the population in the national cause."[10]

To Reymont, Kosciuszko embodied the truly national spirit of the peasantry. Originally Reymont had planned to make him the central character but, as we have seen earlier, the concept of the trilogy changed in the writing, and Reymont focused on his fictional protagonist and his adventures at the expense of historical faithfulness. Kosciuszko is mentioned frequently in the first volume, and emerges more realistically as a military leader in the third, against the ambitious and bold panorama of the battle at Raclawice; he appears in *Nil Desperandum* only in a series of brief sketches, more like a savior of the nation than a real person. Accordingly, he is described metaphorically, in terms related to his superhuman task and spiritual ordeal; his historical role and spiritual experiences are emphasized. We see him as he "raised his very sad eyes, fainting in painful hesitation as if returning from Golgotha"; "he first made a humble sacrifice of himself and having joyfully lifted his cross, he hopefully entered the national road to Calvary"; "when he returned to his comrades he was like Moses stepping down from

Sinai with the tablets of the Commandments, full of fire, majesty, and holiness; he appeared to their eyes as the fiery bush speaking with a voice of incomprehensible fate," and so on. These scriptural metaphors foreshadow Kosciuszko's role in the insurrection as the chosen leader, conscious of his responsibility before the people. The metaphors change in the next volume when he undertakes the command and steps down, as it were, into a more realistic dimension, talking to his soldiers like a popular leader and a beloved general.

The change in the author's original plan is also reflected in the structure of the novel. Kosciuszko is always present in the conversations and plans, but he occupies a secondary place in the plot. It is Zareba who ties together various characters, situations, and changes of scene until the climactic moment of the outbreak of the insurrection. Just as in the first part of the trilogy, the plot links a multitude of people and places into an overall picture of the country on the eve of a daring period of uneven struggle with an enemy whose numbers, armaments, and power are overwhelming. The few months between September 1793 and March 1794 in *Nil Desperandum* are devoted to the preparation for war. Reymont leads his protagonist from a peaceful country estate to the conspirators' headquarters in Warsaw and eventually to Paris, where Zareba contacts the French revolutionaries whose support he was to secure. With Zareba we enter secret gatherings and public balls, we listen to the conversations in the streets and in the salons, we see street beggars and a king. Although his role is often simply that of guide, his personal problems become plot material.

His love affair with Iza is complicated by the introduction of his cousin, Cesia, who is in love with the young conspirator but, being a masculine type of girl, does not want to reveal her feelings openly, she even appears quarrelsome when they meet at the Zarebas. Incidentally, Cesia, like many characters in Reymont's novels, is modeled on a Sienkiewicz character, a successful tomboy, Baska, in *Pan Michael*; such a similarity of type represents another case of the author's closely following his great predecessor's footsteps in an attempt to create an equally popular historical novel. But Reymont is much more aware than Sienkiewicz of social problems; they are underscored even in Zareba's personal story. When the novel opens, we meet him at his father's estate along with Kacper, his orderly and companion, who is recovering from wounds inflicted by the Russians. Kacper is sill considered a serf by the Zarebas, although his military endeavors should have given him the status of a free citizen. He is in love with Zareba's sister, and in spite of Zareba's approval and friendship, this affair creates a serious conflict. The old squire firmly believes in the traditional social order. Upon discovering the romance, he is outraged and intends to beat Kacper up. "I am a soldier. I am a free man," exclaims Kacper trying to get free. The ensuing violent scene between Zareba and his father results in Zareba's banishment, apparently forever.

These two subplots climax in one of the most memorable scenes in the novel. When the dying old squire summons his son several months later, he offers to pardon him if he will marry Cesia. Zareba obeys and the engagement takes place during an impromptu party staged by a jolly invasion of a group of neighbors. One of the best written scenes in the trilogy, the gaiety and cheerfulness of the dancers at the party contrasts with the somber solitude of the old squire, aware of approaching death. He encourages his guests to dance and to drink, as he slowly dies, listening to familiar melodies and watching the merry crowd with his weakening eyes. The lyricism of this scene, enhanced by the colorful description of the ball and the dances, much like the famous ones in *The Peasants,* reveals Reymont's mastery in his mature period at permeating the most dramatic scenes with poetic overtones and making them uniquely impressive.

The balls in *Nil Desperandum,* the picnics, dinners, and parties sparkle with sophisticated conversations, humor, and courtly manners, and largely contribute to that novel's artistic success. Such colorful scenes attracted many writers including Zeromski, whose novel, *The Ashes,* also recaptures the atmosphere of the last days of the doomed nation.

Although Reymont apparently preferred country life to urban, with its emerging bourgeois middle class, he felt equally at ease in describing almost any environment. He had compassion and sympathy for the tradesmen, shoemakers, printers, and people in the streets, all of whom gradually enter the novel as the patriotic conspiracy embraces wider and wider circles. Reymont recreated a full panorama of Polish society at the end of the eighteenth century with an extreme care and an understanding of its basic problems, and with patriotic feeling which is particularly evident when contrasted with his views on France and Frenchmen. The French are presented as being gloomy and repulsive. In a long chapter which hardly belongs to the plot, Zareba travels to Paris, where he seeks a meeting with Robespierre to gain French support for the insurrection. Even though his attempt to speak to the French leader fails, he has an ample opportunity to make comparisons about the French and Polish revolutions and draw conclusions on the differences for himself, and the authorities back in Poland.

The chapter begins, "Paris was dissolving in the foul autumn weather, and in the dirty rags of fog." The suggestion of foulness permeates the scenes of the city and its inhabitants. In spite of the author's attempt to fill Zareba with enthusiasm at the execution of Philippe-Égalité, the effect is rather his disgust at the city and its mood. Zareba, who had dreamed about a similarly radical outcome of the revolution in the streets of Warsaw, grows disillusioned and weary, and his idealism turns to a cynical and sarcastic appraisal of the reality he sees around him. Apparently, pressures of the political ideologies surrounding Reymont began to influence his novel, even though he was determined to make his protagonist a hardboiled revolutionary. Reymont also involuntarily transferred to Zareba his own alienation from Paris which had built up during all those years he spent there. In an earlier novelette, *The Dreamer*, this attitude toward Paris was manifested quite explicitly; but here it is implicit. Although he tried to suppress his feelings as an expatriate writer, the descriptions of the streets filled with singing crowds, the revolutionary mood of the people, the vignettes of the Frenchmen in cafés, restaurants, or in the streets all create the same profound sense of estrangement that exists in many of Reymont's urban novels, including *The Vampire*, which captures the atmosphere of London with an almost Dostoevskyan gloom and intensity.

The contrast between Reymont's attitude toward foreign cities and his native land becomes especially evident in the chapter immediately following Zareba's trip, in which the New Year's celebration of 1794 is described in an exuberantly rich procession of colors and lights through one of the principal streets in Warsaw. In spite of the hostile reception from the crowds gathered on the sidewalks, the long line of politicians, aristocrats, and nobility going to the King's castle with congratulations sparkles; the splendor and dignity of the scene capture the reader's imagination. We cannot but admire the glamour of the ruling circles; we are aware of their moral decay—the shouts from the crowd remind us about their vices— and their pitiful ineffectuality in the hands of foreign powers but the sight is so impressive that we cannot believe that such a fantastically rich country could perish or turn into the gloom of France. The doom hanging over the city notwithstanding, Warsaw is gay and colorful, careless in its joys, and still exciting, hopeful. And as if trying to explore to the limit that desperately carefree mood of those who are about to die in the oncoming war either as victims or as victors, Reymont introduces a surprisingly bold love scene between Zareba and Iza, his former mistress. The scene achieves a perfect union between Reymont's style and action in an image of a nightride of the lovers in a sledge, pulled by demonic horses through snowy fields. This episode, followed by the lover's contempt for himself and for the young woman, who had been a concubine of the Russian officers, adds an element which the novel generally lacks—that purely human passion which is always present in The Peasants and which contributes to that novel's greatness.

This scene rounds out the picture of life in the country on the eve of an eventful hour. The tension which gradually progresses with the novel and the skillful blending of the adventures of the protagonist with the destinies of the nation come to a climax in a memorable scene at a party with news of the outbreak of the insurrection. So powerful are the emotions aroused by the news that even the cynical and lighthearted

Woyna, Zareba's friend, is overwhelmed and loses his custom-
ary detachment. In the silence of surprise, he boldly sings *La
Marseillaise*, the symbol of the ultimate fight everybody has
been expecting.

III   *The Insurrection*

The outbreak of Kosciuszko's insurrection marked one of the
most glorious chapters in Poland's history. After the humiliating
Diet of 1793, when the country was practically sold to the
Russians by the corrupt aristocracy, "the honor of Poland was
saved by the insurrection of the following year," according to
Oscar Halecki.[11] A year of careful preparation resulted not only
in a well-organized conspiracy, but, more importantly, in the
psychological readiness of the nation to overthrow the invaders
and to restore the freedom granted but not fulfilled by the
Constitution of the Third of May in 1791. To grant the constitutional rights of citizens, to abolish serfdom for those who
took up arms, and to punish those who were guilty of treason
were among the main goals of the insurgents. With these goals
the revolutionaries sought to secure the support of the lower
classes and to turn the insurrection into a national uprising
against the foreign and domestic oppressors.

These aims are at the center of the third part of Reymont's
trilogy, which he had planned carefully from the very outset.
As early as 1911, eight years after completing the novel, he
read to an audience in Paris a fragment, "The Death of the
Primate, August 11-12, 1794,"[12] which extends chronologically
beyond the scope of *Insurekcja* (The Insurrection), covering
the period between March 22 and April 18, 1794. Extraliterary
reasons, among which could have been the fear of pressing the
revolutionary issue too hard, an issue which, in 1917 when the
novel was completed, certainly could not have been popular in
Poland, made Reymont end *The Insurrection* with the scene of
a temporary victory over the Russians in the streets of Warsaw.
Nonetheless, the novel possesses sufficient historical exactness
and artistic value to be considered an important achievement.

Compared to the preceding volumes, *The Insurrection* reverses basic elements of composition. The plot and fictional characters become secondary, while historical events are depicted with powerful strength. In this bloody period in Polish history, with the country's fate at stake, decisions were made on the battle-fields rather than in diplomatic negotiations, and so Reymont also changed the setting, and decided to try creating battle pieces according to the best tradition in Polish fiction. Scattered throughout the novel, they vary in setting, character, and intensity but are always in the foreground. During the four weeks of the novel's action more fighting takes place than in the two preceding novels, which were mostly devoted to preparations for the war and a few skirmishes in which Zareba proved his bravery rather than his wisdom. Among the fight scenes the presentation of the battle at Raclawice is the most impressive, followed by numerous scenes of street fighting in Warsaw. Reymont had waited until this third volume and proved his creative power in the field so far occupied only by his famous predecessors.

The insurrection is introduced with a scene in the ruins of an old abbey at Tyniec, where a group of volunteers have gathered in readiness for combat. In vivid colloquial conversations among the soldiers, Reymont depicts the spirit of those on whose shoulders the success of the uprising heavily rests. Comparison with a French crowd of revolutionaries in *Nil Desperandum* reveals the Frenchmen as a violent and uncontrollable force, bloodthirsty and uncouth, and the Polish volunteers as soldiers, honest, aware of their goal, determined to fight for liberty. With a few strokes of the pen each character is individualized: some are funny, some lazy, some simply all-too-human in their desire for food or a pair of shoes. There is not enough food, to be sure, and the military discipline is lax, but even so the volunteers are conscientious freedom fighters, and their spirit is high.

When Kosciuszko takes personal command, he is presented in more realistic terms than in the previous novel, a leader committed to chivalry in warfare. When told about a futile effort to take the Russian garrison in Cracow by surprise, he reproves an officer saying:

"Our duty is to rise in the bright daylight, openly, beating the drums. The cause for which we are ready to give our necks does not fear the light, and to attack the enemy by guile would not suit it. A Pole has always despised ambushes, and God forbid that he should change. We shall not fail to have enough strength to defeat our enemies if we do not fail to have the spirit of sacrifice and love."[13]

This is the lofty Kosciuszko, the savior of the previous novel; to make him *Naczelnik,* the national leader, and a more human character Reymont shows him, like Shakespeare's Henry V, in several conversations with the soldiers among whom he walks unrecognized. His Christ-like qualities persist, however, even in these simple talks. Kosciuszko ends his night watch, for example, by comparing his soldiers with the Crusaders protecting Christianity, and concludes with a thought which is to become the leading theme in the novel: "A free peasant means free Poland, for he is the foundation of her greatness and independence."[14]

With these words Kosciuszko disappears into the rainy night, but his presence is constantly kept in the foreground in the following chapters. We witness his tormenting solitude when he makes his fateful decision to take full responsibility for the insurrection. We are with him in the town square in Cracow when he takes an oath granting civil rights to the peasants and limiting their serfdom. We accompany him through the battle at Raclawice, the first important success of the insurrection. Although in the novel Zareba and several fictional characters from the preceding volumes participate in the battle, evidently it is Kosciuszko who captures the author's imagination; a real hero, he proves to be more dramatic than any imaginary character.

The battle at Raclawice, fought on April 4, 1794 against the Russian regiments under General Tormasov, occupies a special place in Polish history. Small, compared to other pitched battles, its significance was more ideological than military: it was the first time that the peasant volunteers scored a major victory over the Russian regulars. Bartosz Glowacki, who captured a cannon with his bare hands, became a national hero and a symbol of the new breed of freedom-fighters. Hundreds of other peasant volunteers won fame through their courage and gallant endeavors, transferring the tradition of chivalry from the nobility to the newly emerging class of patriots of peasant stock. Naturally, their appearance as a decisive factor in national life at this time generally acknowledged by the historians, was important for Reymont. To create a memorable battle scene without imitating those of Sienkiewicz, Zeromski, and other Polish novelists was not an easy task, but Reymont succeeded. First he depicted the parade of troops moving into the field, presenting each unit separately and creating at the same time a powerful stream of thousands of people in motion; eventually he focused on his ordinary heroes, instead of either the commanding officers or the fictional characters of the battle. Such a method called for mass scenes rather than setting individuals against the background of the fight. And here Reymont's imagery, always responsive to the movement of masses, came to the fore. He presented the two armies as two mighty elements clashing with immense impact, crushing and destroying each other. As a most appropriate stylistic device he used metaphors and similes related to nature, since only the power of elements could stand comparison with the fury and determination of the fighting. Paragraphs contain such figures of speech as, "they ran into each other with the ferocity of hungry wolves," "there were terrifying whirls in which one could see only bloody bayonets and sabres," "men were falling heavily like trees cut down," and "the roars of pain streamed as fountains of blood," etc. The heavy use of adjectives and adverbs, by now typical of Reymont's style, creates an almost sensual impression, which complements the imagery. Reymont, like Zeromski in similar scenes, concentrated on creating visual impressions rather than human and psychological experience. It was, incidentally, a method familiar in Polish historical fiction, which had always relied on an emotional, intense style rather than on the detached objectivity of Tolstoy or Stephen Crane's psychological introspection.

Equally impressionistic and broad are the novel's final scenes of fighting in the streets of Warsaw. The masses of soldiers and insurgents, entangled in combat in the narrow passages and courtyards of the Old Town, defend and fight for single houses and even rooms with the fury of the elements and the roar of thunder. Into these scenes Reymont brings almost all the characters who have appeared in the trilogy, along with a multitude of historical figures, and thus creates the sense of a whole nation involved in an ultimate struggle for survival. *The Insurrection* pays proper tribute to those gallant soldiers whose spirit was best recaptured in the song written in 1797 by Jozef Wybicki and later adopted as Poland's national anthem, "Poland is not yet lost."

With such a broad conception of the novel's climax in mind, Reymont paid much less attention to Zareba and the plot concerning the protagonist than in the first two novels. Zareba fights and personally carries Kosciuszko's orders to the troops at Raclawice, but his story becomes less and less important in the broader scope of *The Insurrection*. Hence the two scenes in which he does play a major role do not create the intended effect, although taken out of the context, they are among the most significant scenes in Zareba's story. In the first Zareba is summoned to a secret conference, and to his surprise discovers he has to face the King himself, in an open discussion. The conflict between his duty to obey his supreme commander, supreme even though ousted by the insurrection, and his devotion to the revolutionary cause could have resulted in a penetrating psychological study of a man torn betwen his obligations and his convictions. But Reymont let the conflict evaporate, and the promising scene ends with a lukewarm conversation and the author's noncommittal remark, "And their talk lasted long through the night."

In the second scene Zareba boldly opposes the death sentence pronounced upon the King at the secret gathering of the Masonic Order. Again there is no convincing psychological motivation for the contrast between the lonely protagonist and the rest of the conspirators, who talk more like puppets than people, using clichés and theatrical declamation. Compared to the powerful presentation of the Freemason movement and rituals which are intrinsically woven into Zeromski's *The Ashes*, Reymont's scene is a superficial ornament to the conspiracy. We also feel that

carried away by the stream of historical events the novelist lost
interest in the fictional plot.

Since the trilogy remained unfinished, it is understandable
that Reymont did not solve all the problems he introduced in
the plot. Zareba is left holding Iza in his arms in a burning
street of Warsaw, and after finishing *The Insurrection* the
reader does not know or care what will happen to them. By
then he is more involved in the nation's ultimate struggle than in
fictional characters. Thus the fiction has moved into the realm
of history, into its real drama, often more poignant than the story
of imaginary characters. And if Reymont's trilogy is a partial
failure because of its uneven structure and some minor faults, the
author achieved something perhaps more important than literary perfection, an impressive image of bygone days, and created
a feeling of classical catharsis of national emotions by evoking
the glory of the past.

CHAPTER 8

The Dreamer *and the Psychopaths*

I The Dreamer

THE long novels did not entirely occupy Reymont's creative
mind. Between publication of the last volume of *The
Peasants* in 1909 and 1911, when he began to publish *The Year
1794*, he brought out three volumes of shorter fiction, a novel
Wampir (Vampire), a narrative *Z Ziemi chelmskiej* (From the
Chelm Territory), devoted to the Russians' persecution of the
Uniate Church in Poland, and a collection of short stories
including a novelette, *Marzyciel* (The Dreamer) (1910).

The roots of the novelette are in a short story, "Work!," written
in 1891, at the beginning of Reymont's literary apprenticeship.
The protagonist of that early story, Jan Balinski, an unemployed
clerk, visits an old friend who is dying of tuberculosis. After
enjoying his hospitality for a considerable period, Jan begins to
experience an overwhelming feeling of jealousy and envy for
his friend's secure social position and eventually murders him
in order to get his job. When it is given to someone else, Jan
commits suicide, illustrating the rather simple moral lesson that
crime does not pay. The value of "Work!" lies not in its sim-
plistic philosophy but in its realistic presentation of an individual's revolt against society set in a provincial railroad station
where the daily routine of trains and schedules creates an atmosphere of boredom and futility. The struggle in Jan's mind is
enhanced by the environment of petty bourgeoisie, where pedestrian problems, gossip, and despair evoke the wildest ideas and
ambitions in the newcomer eventually leading to murder and
suicide.

This conflict between an individual and the overpowering
pressure of the provincial life against which he revolts in vain is

119

further developed in both novels about Janka Orlowska, but only in *The Dreamer* does it achieve full dimension and receive appropriate artistic form, purged of incidental motifs. Centered in the foreground, it becomes the theme of the novelette.

The story is obviously based on the author's experiences, but it is above all a work of fiction. Although Reymont certainly put many of his own sympathies and phobias into *The Dreamer*, the action of which coincides with the author's most unhappy years, as if he wanted to get rid of the nightmarish world of provincial existence by reviving them in Jozio's sufferings, the protagonist, Jozio, should be considered purely fictional.

The setting of the story in the railroad station has far-reaching implications. Even in the most remote towns, the station represents the outside world, almost a symbolic connecting point between the reality of daily existence and that of dreams. The railroad station is a favorite locale in fiction and the pictorial arts, including cinematography. In Russia, for instance, a country with immense distances between human settlements, the station was a social center, a meeting place of provincial society, and the place where one could glimpse a different kind of person passing by in the cars like personifications of dreams about a different kind of life. In Alexander Kuprin's novel *The Duel* (1905), for example, the daydreaming protagonist, Romashov, used to go to the station just to pretend that he was a dashing young officer, to look at the elegant passengers on an express-train and from those brief moments he fed his dreams, which replaced his dreary existence. Kuprin's novel deserves special attention in relation to Reymont's story. *The Duel* appeared in a Polish translation in 1906, and since it was a best seller, it must have been known to Reymont. Although *The Dreamer* is primarily derived from the novelist's own experience, there is an interesting parallel between the two stories as well as a certain similarity between the authors, especially in their artistic unevenness. The harsh judgment pronounced on Kuprin by D. S. Mirsky could be applied to Reymont at his worst:

He was torn between various tendencies. Being essentially a man of no culture, he could not really profit from any literary example;

and, possessing very little artistic tact, he could not distinguish between what was good in his writings and what was bad.[1]

Reymont's version of the provincial dreamer is also close to Russian literary tradition, perhaps even closer than to Polish fiction. The dominating tone of the story is foreign to Polish literary tradition and can best be defined by the Russian term *poshlost'*. In his study on Chekhov, who almost made that term a key to the general mood of many of his stories, Thomas Winner defines it as follows:

A persuasive Chekhovian theme, already implied in many of the stories discussed, is that of a conflict between beauty and the elusive quality expressed by the Russian term *poshlost'*. This untranslatable term connotes vulgarity, banality, poor taste, superficial values, conceit, and dilletantism. . . . Many of Chekhov's sensitive souls suffocate in the surrounding of *poshlost'*.[2]

Although Jozio Pelka, the protagonist of *The Dreamer*, can be hardly described as a Chekhovian sensitive soul, he literally suffocates in the provincial atmosphere and can find escape only in his daydreams. In this he resembles Kuprin's Romashov except that his dreams mostly concentrate on a specific form of escape, travelling abroad. His obsession with that dream becomes pathological: in an attempt to turn his dreams into reality, he disguises himself as an Englishman and goes on a week-end to Warsaw pretending to be a foreigner without any understanding of Polish. The portrayal of the obsession is so intense, incidentally, that Reymont does not explore the obvious possibilities for making that scene comical and emphasizes only Jozio's frustrations. Another one of his dreams centers on a beautiful girl on an express-train, who becomes for Jozio a "princess"; in a futile attempt to rescue her from a train stranded in a blizzard he experiences another bitter awakening when his pseudo-heroic deed is confronted with the sober reality of his low social position and hence the complete indifference of "the princess." After these failures he turns to heavy drinking to escape from the disappointments and the *poshlost'* of his vulgar love affair with a possessive woman, his poverty, and the boredom of provincial existence.

There is, however, another escape, and Reymont finds a
simple solution. Money can rescue Jozio from his psychological
torments. Suddenly Jozio's mind, possessed by the idea of becoming rich, begins to work on that problem with tremendous
intensity. *The Dreamer*, originally conceived as a psychological
study, eventually also becomes a crime novel in the best tradition of that genre, exploring the motives of the crime, the
hesitation beforehand, and even the repentance. Driven by
powerful desire, Jozio steals money from a friend who had
received a grant to study in Paris and then, filled with remorse,
returns it, but the idea of stealing sticks in his mind. An unsuc-
cessful attempt to borrow money from a pawnbroker results
in a conversation which leads to a new project, embezzling
cash from the railroad office. Jozio substitutes for the cashier
at the station and cannot resist the temptation. He pockets a
substantial sum of rubles and sets out for Paris.

Jozio spat at the station through the window with an unspeakable
contempt and hatred, and having sat down on a bench in the corridor
he closed his eyes and let himself be carried away by a mad joy.
Thus ended his bad dream about life and the reality he yearned for
began.[3]

Jozio's "mad joy" over his liberation achieved through crime,
and his double identity are reminiscent of Dostoevsky's pathological characters. In "The Theme of the Double in Dostoevsky," Dmitri Cizevskij points out that Golyadkin, in *The
Double* "has no place of his own, he has never achieved one in
his life, he has no sphere of his own in life except possibly the
corner behind the cupboard or the stove where he hides from
the imaginary persecutions of his enemies."[4] It is evident that
both authors, although they differed philosophically, in a great
many respects had a common interest in psychopathology.
In Dostoevsky's novels, however, the double is the embodiment of a twisted psyche carried to the extreme; Reymont does
not go so far, he merely shows an unhappy human being searching for another ego. Even so, Jozio's twisted mind ceases to distinguish between dream and reality in a story filled with all
the paraphernalia typical of Dostoevsky's novels—crime, em-

bezzlement, drinking, boredom, and an inevitable tragic end.

From the beginning of The Dreamer one might expect the fulfillment of the dream to be happiness, if only as a contrast to the gloomy existence Jozio had been leading at the provincial station. But Reymont was too good a psychologist for such a conclusion. The foreign countries for which Jozio yearned prove to be completely disappointing. In Paris Jozio finds consolation only in continuing his dreams. Looking at the grand avenues, he feels discouraged by the elegant crowds, the noise, and the monstrous pace of life in the big city. To escape that new reality, he turns the people around him into characters from the romances. "He found himself in his own element because he was able to make his dreams real, to have the reality he had always yearned for." Whenever he has to face reality, he compares it with his imagination and keeps repeating to himself, "No. This is not it, this is not." Subsequently, he dreams of quiet life at the station, and he idealizes the daily routine and even the boredom. The disillusionments and homesickness make his life unbearable, and when the police begin to search for him as a criminal, Jozio in despair concludes that "everything is a lie, even a dream," throws himself under an oncoming train and dies.

The Dreamer has been generally misinterpreted. Julian Krzyzanowski dismisses the story as concerning "a man who, indeed, after a petty crime wound up in a Paris gutter,"[5] although he approves of the realistic presentation of provincial life and the stuffy atmosphere of the railroad station. Most critics either completely disregard the story or dismiss it with a few remarks. For Reymont, however, The Dreamer was an ambitious and meaningful attempt to write a psychological novel about the problems of identity of a man who cannot distinguish between reality and fancy, a man who is obsessed with the idea of transgressing the limits of his pitiful existence. A careful comparison of The Dreamer with twentieth-century novels created under the impact of scientific discoveries and psychology suggests that Reymont correctly anticipated the new direction in psychological fiction of our age; beneath the surface of a seemingly sensational crime story he meant to show a psychological analysis of an obsessed individual. Reymont set out to investigate the unknown in the human mind. Turning his interest toward psychology and pathology, he pointed out some new vistas for many of his contemporaries.

II   The Vampire

This attraction toward abnormal psychology had two sources in Reymont's life. His youthful experience with spiritualistic circles in Poland and in England was eventually strengthened by the trend at the turn of the century toward a "scientific" explanation of human destinies and the existence of life beyond the grave. Numerous intellectuals, scientists, and artists, not to mention the general public, devoted much effort to obtaining proofs of the supernatural, which they often took very seriously. Innumerable movements, societies, and pseudo-religious sects emerged; often they were open invitations to bold impostors who frequently succeeded in convincing whole groups of believers of their supernatural powers, particularly in their "communication" with the world beyond.

Reymont returned to his youthful interest in spiritualism around 1904, but did not complete *The Vampire* until 1910. One has a feeling that the renowned author, exhausted from completing *The Peasants*, was desperately searching for new themes, and began to dig into his memories for material. Between *The Peasants* and the historical trilogy he wrote a semi-journalistic account of the persecution of the Uniates and two short novels: *The Dreamer*, closely related to his adolescent years, and *The Vampire*, in which he attempted to recreate some of his memories of experiences related to the new public interest in the supernatural. Perhaps it was the failure of both these novels which made Reymont change his mind and undertake the laborious study which was needed to turn to historical fiction; perhaps it was his realization that he was not at ease with contemporary novels—at any rate, this period marked a low ebb of his creative power. It must be noted, however, that he was very serious in his belief in spiritualism and took an active part in its practices to the last years of his life. As late as 1917 he participated in a

seance with a well-known Polish psychologist, Julian Ochoro-
wicz, and two internationally famous mediums, Domanski and
Guzik.[6]

The idea of combining his own first-hand observation with
spiritualistic theory in a work of fiction had fascinated Reymont for some time. In *The Vampire* he used the notes he had
made in London in 1894 and a sketch published in 1903, "In
Fog," which deals with spiritualism, hypnosis, and supernatural
powers. To these he added the plot of an early sketch for a drama,
Too Late, abandoned after an amateur performance in Paris
in 1899.[7] Although these various autobiographical and fictional
materials seemed particularly suitable for the decadent taste
of the first decade of the century, enamored of the metaphysical
and mystifying, the novel was a complete failure. Today it is
interesting primarily for what it tells us about Reymont and
his epoch.

The story concerns a mysterious gentleman, Zenon, who
lives in a London boardinghouse populated by a collection of
strange characters. Zenon spends most of his time wandering
about the city as if in a trance, not knowing who he is or what
he is doing. The reader does not learn until very late that Zenon
is a Polish author who had left his country and settled down in
England as Mr. Walter Brown, a novelist. This information consequently leads to the disclosure of Zenon's very elaborate love
affair back in Poland and subsequently to a symbolic fight
between good and evil powers for Zenon's soul.

Early in the novel Zenon runs nervously about the city,
crossing innumerable streets searching for the meaning of life.
These walks with the author's realistic observations of London
presented in a dense aura of fog, rain, and despair hanging over
the metropolis are the only artistically valuable parts of the
novel. Against that somber background Reymont's impressive
pictures of people and places come close to Dostoevsky's *Winter Notes on Summer Impressions* in their general criticism of
social conditions in England and the image of a foreigner lost
in a London night with its poverty, crime, and pathos.

Zenon's observations on London and on English society are
projected against the background of his internal struggle. At

the boardinghouse he has met and fallen under the inexplicable spell of a mysterious Miss Daisy, who is always accompanied by a wild panther. In spite of his lovely, goodhearted fiancée's efforts, he drifts closer and closer to that fearful stranger. Reymont underscores the contrast between the two women by the different colors associated with them. In scenes with Betsy, the fiancée, there are mostly warm, bright tones and the narrative flows smoothly without interruption, in simple traditional phrases. Daisy, to the contrary, appears either in dim light or in dark, somber colors; in her scenes the style changes to a series of short, nervous exclamations in a stream of abrupt sentences and unfinished phrases. The dark tone takes over when Zenon is carried away by the terrifying whirl of new experiences to the final triumph of evil forces.

Daisy proves to be a vampire who "puts on any shape in order to devour souls." When she fails to capture her victim in an orgiastic rite which Satan attends, she casts an evil spell on Zenon's natural daughter. In spite of the combined efforts of his fiancée and his former mistress who join in the fight against the vampire, Zenon refuses to be helped and departs with Daisy "in an unknown direction."

All this sounds today like a lot of cheap nonsense, but it was in keeping with the spirit of the epoch which had a decisive impact on the novelist who wanted to create a "modern" novel which appealed to the public taste. Most certainly, *The Vampire* does not occupy any important place among Reymont's works; like a great majority of novels of that period it is now practically unreadable. The stylistic conventions of Modernism with its topical interest make the novel often unpalatable and sometimes ridiculous. It is more evidence of the author's following of literary fashion with an almost complete disregard for his artistic integrity, or a lack of a solid philosophical background and consequently a philosophy of art.

Some critics did consider *The Vampire* to be a document of a spiritual crisis of the contemporary mind; however, because of its artistic unevenness, the general reception was cool. Reymont himself was dissatisfied with the work and soon turned to historical fiction. Nonetheless, his vivid interest in psychology and spiritualism resulted in symbolistic and mystical short stories which expressed his concern for the meaning of life in a new form. The irrational began to replace the real, as he began to concentrate on issues for which he could not find a rational solution. For at about that time decisive changes were beginning to occur in Polish society.

CHAPTER 9

Against Revolutions

EVEN a superficial look at the history of Polish literature leads inevitably to the conclusion that it almost always has been politically motivated. Western writers, working in an atmosphere of freedom, could reflect philosophical, intellectual, and social trends in their fiction while mainly devoting their creative powers to achieving artistic perfection. In Poland, however, due to her tumultuous history, almost every major novel or poem has a pronounced political background. Artistic values should not, of course, be disregarded, but in order to understand Polish literature fully, one must consider political and historical factors. Mickiewicz's *Pan Tadeusz* or Prus's *The Doll*, two outstanding examples of Polish nineteenth-century poetry and fiction respectively, are undoubtedly literary masterpieces, but analyzed in their historical context they also reveal a concern for extra-literary problems that preoccupied contemporary minds and, to a great extent, influenced them. Such an approach does not imply the narrow sociological interpretation of the Marxist Socialist Realistic critics—it simply serves to enrich our understanding of the complex history of Polish literature.

Reymont stayed away from the political problems of his epoch as long as he could. Remote in time from the heavy burden of Romantic Messianism of the first half of the nineteenth century, and hardly influenced by the Positivistic social purposefulness of its second half, he did not consider a work of literature as a vehicle for a patriotic or social message, much less as an expression of a political creed. In the major novels of his mature period, *The Promised Land* and the first two parts of *The Peasants*, he deliberately avoided politics. But as time progressed his own political views began to consolidate, partly for extra-

128

literary reasons, such as pressures from National Democrats eager to convert the novelist to their ideology, and partly because he realized that as a major literary figure, he could not ignore the main issues of his country. Eventually, the artist submitted to the patriot, for whom Poland's national independence became the most essential question.

The Revolution of 1905 did more than shake the Russian Empire. While in Russia it meant a breakdown of certain historical traditions, and eventually dramatically changed the course of Russian history, in Poland the Revolution was mainly reflected in the fulfillment of hopes which the captive country had been treasuring for more than a century. The crumbling Russian colossus was about to collapse, and a new free Poland might emerge from its ruins. And although the modern Polish historians follow the Marxist interpretation of that period and emphasize the class struggle as its main issue, an objective approach reveals the patriotic spirit as a main issue in the Revolution of 1905 in Poland. The revolutionary workers, led by the Polish Socialist Party, P. P. S., representing the avant-garde of the whole revolutionary movement, were motivated at least as much by patriotism as by class consciousness. The combination of these revolutionary and patriotic elements at times turned the revolution in Poland into a general upheaval against the Russians. Later, when the P. P. S. consolidated to become the decisive force in the Polish patriotic movement, Jozef Pilsudski and his military legion emerged from its ranks and subsequently formed the army which was to secure Poland's independence in 1918, and to protect her against the Soviet invasion in 1920.

Reymont now was mostly interested in the national character of the Revolution of 1905. In a journalistic sketch, "From the Constitutional Days," written and published during the riots, he carefully balanced the patriotic and social aspects of the events he had witnessed in Warsaw. He saw that it was the proletariat who was pressing for revolutionary issues and desperately fighting for social betterment, while the bourgeois elements remained either passive, terrified, or even hostile to the events taking place in the streets. He emphasized the strong contrast between these two groups, juxtaposing the workers who were deprived of work and basic food with the bourgeoisie who lamented the lack of pastries, but characteristically Reymont identified himself with neither group. He merely reported the bloody events objectively, attempting to capture the spirit reigning in the streets, in the cafés, in the whole city shocked by the Revolution.

The Marxists cannot forgive Reymont his impressive images of the spirit of national unity, so contrary to their interpretation of history. Budrecki flatly accuses Reymont of falsifying reality,[1] when in fact, Reymont just described the situation as he saw it develop day by day. Under the date November 1, he records how two groups of demonstrators marched from two different parts of the city. From Wola, an industrial district of Warsaw mostly populated by workers, comes a group with red flags, singing "The Red Banner," the song of the Revolution. From downtown another group of demonstrators marches with Polish national flags, singing the national anthem. "The marchers meet each other, they lower their flags and join hands. 'Long live freedom! Long live Poland!'" An elderly gentleman follows another group, listens to their song and exclaims: "What do they sing? 'The Red Banner.' Good, brothers! God be with you!"[2]

The sketch ends with an impressive picture of the demonstration on November 5 organized by the National Democrats as the climax of the Revolutionary events: the Poles thought they had achieved a partial victory when the Russians granted constitutional rights to the Polish population by way of the Tsar's manifesto. Reymont, unaware of the political game played by the parties, joined the general enthusiasm and did not try to determine the real meaning of the manifesto. He did not realize that, as Oscar Halecki observes, "Tsarism, which at first attempted to appease the rebels by concessions proclaimed by the Constitution of October, 1905, ended, finally, by crushing all opposition."[3]

Reymont's attempt to analyze the psychological motives of the revolutionaries also proved futile. In the same volume of stories and sketches, published in 1907 under the title *Na*

krawedzi (On the Edge), there is a short story, "I Have
Killed," which is intended as a study of guilt based on Revolutionary events and the Socialist movement, apparently P. P. S.
Jedrus Kowalski, a member of an underground organization,
has been selected by his comrades to carry out a political assas-
sination of an undercover agent of the Russian secret police.
Driven by deep ideological convictions and the powerful need
to prove himself worthy of the party's confidence, he sets a
trap and succeeds in assassinating the agent. After that he
remains cool and calm, proud of a deed well done. But that is
just the beginning of his tragedy.

After several days he accidentally encounters a funeral in
the street, and to his growing horror discovers it is his victim's.
A mysterious force draws the assassin to the procession, "as if
some horrible hands extended from that coffin, and pulled him
by his hair." Only after watching the mourning family and the
gloomy ceremony does Jedrus begin to realize what he has done,
not to the traitor but to a human being whom he has annihilated.
His real suffering begins when he realizes his guilt as a common
killer of another man. Remorse and fear overpower him; he
breaks down and almost loses his senses. When he finally finds
his way out of the cemetery and goes to a tavern, he publicly
confesses his guilt, but no one believes him. He is taken for
a madman. Jedrus is left alone, his conscience tormenting him
day and night. Arrested by accident, he is set free as a lunatic
and spends the rest of his life running from "the furies of madness and fear."

This study of the psychology of a killer tries to avoid any
political implications. Although based on real terrorist activities of the P. P. S. during and after the Revolution, the story
does not condemn either the methods or the assassins directly,
but is instead meant as a warning against violence in general,
which Reymont rejected on moral principles. The unbearable
psychological suffering of a human being who commits violence
spoke to him more strongly than any revolutionary slogans. In
his account of the Revolutionary days of Warsaw one scene
testifies to those convictions. In his wandering about town
the narrator, whom we may safely identify as the author, meets

a small procession. The half-naked body of a young Jew killed
by five bullets and a bayonet lies on a cart surrounded by the
members of his family, who "carry him slowly as if he were a
banner of freedom torn in battle." "I will never forget him
until I die," confesses the narrator, leaving no doubt about his
own point of view. It was the reaction of a moralist confronted
with any revolution and its methods.

From the same period, between 1905 and 1907, came two
more stories which document the gradual change in Reymont's
approach to politics. While in 1905 he still seemed carried away
by the fervor of the revolutionary upheaval, in the following
years he grew pessimistic and pensive; revolution began to
appear to his weary eyes as a general disaster, a monstrous
cataclysm equally destructive to its enemies and followers. To
convey this he chose to write impersonally, symbolically, using
images that were supposed to carry general significance. In
powerful metaphors he depicted revolution as universal danger,
threatening the very existence of the human race. Without
defending any particular social order, Reymont expressed his
utmost concern with the destructive forces in society which the
Revolution might unleash. Thus, the stories are removed from
any historical context and become symbols of fearful powers.

In the first one, "On the Edge," a rebellion is being waged
against an anonymous tyrant, significantly named He, who fights
desperately against the masses surrounding his magnificent
castle, who gain strength every day. When the rebels are about
to inflict the final blow, He descends to the secret vaults and sets
free the captured leaders of the revolution. His magnanimous
gesture does not evoke appreciation however; instead, his prison-
ers accuse him of his previous crimes against basic human rights.
As the final disaster approaches, his lieutenants leave him one
one by one. Eventually He is handed over to the revolutionaries.
When the gates of the castle open, He steps out alone against
the mob. By doing so, He achieves the moral victory of a man
who has overcome fear, made peace with himself, and faces
death with calm dignity.

As in "I Have Killed," Reymont is more interested here in
the psychological problems of an individual involved in vio-

lence than in the ideology of revolution. Although the personal
drama of the tyrant takes place against a multi-colored background of revolution described with the grandiloquence and
emotional exaggeration typical of Reymont's style in that period,
the author shows clearly that his main interest is the human
soul entangled in the moral conflict resulting from violence.
Reymont refrains from taking any overt political stand; he is
even reluctant to pass any moral judgement. He does underscore the personal courage of the tyrant who has overcome his
faults, who repudiates them and faces punishment with dignity,
thus emerging a real victor.

Unfortunately the form of that story is hardly appropriate
for a convincing human drama. Stripped of realistic features,
the story's fairy-tale atmosphere is saturated with rather meaningless symbolism more typical of a gothic tale than a psychological drama. The final message dissolves into a maze of chaotic
impressions created by the fantastic, supernatural character of
the rebellion considered, as it were, a mysterious force of ultimate destruction. This was in keeping with Reymont's new point
of view; he began to regard revolution as a cataclysm disastrous
to the basic moral values sustaining the life of a society. The
story ends with an impressive image of death reigning over the
world. Clearly, for Reymont the periods of hope and enthusiasm were over. The scars inflicted in 1905 must have been
deeper than his first impressions had revealed, and only in the
next years did they begin to appear in Reymont's fiction.

"The Graveyard," written in 1906 in Paris and published in
the same collection as the stories discussed above, is to some
extent more realistic than "On the Edge." In its symbolism and
structure, "The Graveyard" is closest to these stories, although
it has the same subject as *The Promised Land*. An account of a
workers' strike in an industrial metropolis, it turns into an apocalyptic vision of destruction, destruction inflicted by the strikers
first on the factories, then on the city, and eventually upon the
whole world. After the revolution the city turns into ruins
slowly devoured by nature. Finally, the human race is able
to revive and to live wisely, "without violence, without false-
hood, without crime," although we never learn from the story

how such idealistic people have evolved. The factories, deserted and destroyed, have become for the survivors "the monuments of the devilish time of reign of injustice, egoism, gold, and violence."

This striking antiurbanism is the result of Reymont's general attitude toward industrial cities revealed earlier in *The Promised Land* and strengthened by the shock of the Revolution of 1905. The industrial novel and these short stories taken together suggest a profound suspicion of urban life and its repercussions on individuals, particularly workers, whom Reymont regarded as victims of industrialization rather than conscientious fighters for a new social order. The accusatory tone of "The Graveyard" is aimed against "the centers of evil" in a powerful vision of their ultimate destruction. Once again, as a Neo-Romantic, Reymont idealized natural life as opposed to the dreary existence in cities, with lofty disregard for reality and the economic laws of human progress.

It is interesting to compare the stylistic devices used to depict the city in *The Promised Land* with those in this story written ten years later. In the novel, factories often became giant animals; here these are depicted in such metaphors as "red nightmares shining in the sunshine as if turned into stone with blood and sweat," "monstrous polypi having grown on the labors of whole generations at the expense of their souls, the air, the earth, and the whole nature," "stony monsters," "temples of a terrible god to whom the human race had to sacrifice its blood," and the like. Instead of animating the factories, Reymont gave them a new dimension of horror and monstrosity, clearly revealing his attitude in these expressionistic images. Throughout the story the realism of the novel has been converted into intensive symbolism, casting everything in an unreal, nightmarish light in which real objects dissolve into a haze of terror and violence. This is in full accord with the author's vision of the world after the revolution: "Everything has achieved the contours of hallucination, everything seems to be drowned at the bottom of a dream populated by terrible nightmares and phantoms of incomprehensible things." Stylistically, then, the story is much closer to the illusionary world of *The Vampire* than to *The Promised Land*.

In spite of its pseudo-optimistic ending of universal peace and happiness finally achieved by humanity, Reymont's deep concern with the problems of radical movements is revealed in gloomy and ironic comments scattered throughout the story. In the beginning when the strike upsets the industry, the author seems to be on the workers' side; they introduce to business bookkeeping "an unexpected value: the man appeared, broke his yoke, and demanded his human account." When, however, the strike changes into revolution Reymont comments on that new human factor which has suddenly turned wild: "They killed in the name of freedom. They killed in the name of equality. They killed in the name of brotherhood." This motif, later used in the historical trilogy in the chapter on the French Revolution, indicates that Reymont as a moralist could not overcome his abhorrence of destruction and killing no matter how lofty the slogans. Although he never expressed his view more explicitly, it is evident that Reymont believed in the firm moral standards of Christian ethics which he attempted to embody in his symbolic visions.

His convictions are perhaps given their most impressive artistic form in a parable "The Riot," written as late as 1924 and generally considered his "most politically involved story."[4] Subtitled "a fable," it is an animal allegory. In the time-honored tradition of that genre, Reymont used it as a vehicle to depict revolution and its repercussions on society and the individuals involved. The principal character, a dog significantly named Rex, leads an exodus of domestic and wild animals who seek freedom from human tyranny. Left on their own, they have a series of unfortunate adventures in the wilderness through which they wander toward the wonderland of their dreams. When he cannot find the promised paradise, they revolt again, this time turning against their leader and lynching him. And when they finally decide to submit to human government they cannot find people anymore, and as a substitute for humans they begin to worship a gorilla, begging him to become their master.

The most obvious comparison for the modern reader's memory

is George Orwell's *Animal Farm*, although as in "The Graveyard," once interpreted as "an allegoric vision of the Communist state,"[5] Reymont does not specifically name any particular
state or political system he had in mind while writing this satire
on Communism. Impersonal and symbolic, it lacks the tension
of human drama which related Evgenij Zamyatin's *We* and
Orwell's *1984* so poignantly to the tragedies inherent in the
Communist system. Reymont's story dissolves in grandiloquence
and generalizing symbolism and misses the point, even if only
by a hair. Perhaps it was too early for the Polish author to
realize the imminent evil of Communism which was only emerging at that time from the turmoil of revolution. Even though
he did finally express his views on the Russian Revolution of
1917, he aimed his satire against the idea of revolution rather
than its fulfillment, and his use of allegory to charge actual
events with a broader, more universal meaning, proved to be
a mistake, both ideologically and artistically. The stylistic convention he had unsuccessfully employed in previous stories dealing with revolution, substituted grandiloquence for grandeur
and once more failed to convey the message. While that style
did create a certain pathetic effect in stories concerned with
moral issues, such as "On the Edge" and "The Graveyard,"
in this case the chasm between events presented and implied
meaning was too great to result in an artistically impressive
story. As a result he produced an unfortunate hybrid of an
almost Biblical parable and the anthropomorphic tale typical,
for instance, of Kipling's animal stories. Instead of a political
satire, in its effect "The Riot" is a pamphlet rather than the
vision of an accomplished artist.

In spite of its artistic failure, "The Riot," the last finished work
of Reymont's career, conveys the author's deep conviction that
society as well as the individual should be governed by moral
laws which cannot be transgressed without creating chaos, disaster, and eventually failure. Ironically, Reymont's attempts to
create contemporary works devoted to politics failed, but if
the novelist left any political testament to the turbulent world
emerging from the abysses of war and revolution, it is these
stories.

CHAPTER 10

In the United States

THE mass emigration of Polish peasants to the United States which began in the last quarter of the nineteenth century was from the first well-documented by sociologists and historians on both sides of the Atlantic, in Poland and in America. But Polish writers almost totally ignored the spectacular topic with the dramatic and often tragic stories of people who crossed the ocean to a completely different land, who struggled in the new environment for identity as well as survival, and who finally emerged as a homogeneous ethnic group with an important place in the new society without support or encouragement from their politically nonexistent mother country. Sienkiewicz witnessed some of those personal dramas during his trip to the United States in 1876-79 and wrote of them in his memorable stories, "After Bread" and "The Lighthouse Keeper," but no one dealt in fiction with the whole process of emigration and its complex social and psychological problems.

In 1892 a leading Polish poet, Maria Konopnicka, began a long descriptive poem *Pan Balcer w Brazylii* (Mr. Balcer in Brazil) intended as a heroic epic of the Polish peasants' emigration to South America; however, the poem, completed in 1910, proved an artistic failure despite its ambitious scope and a certain poetic value. This was obviously a topic for an epic novel, not for poetry. It seemed appropriate, then, that such a novel on the problems of emigration should be written by an author who was particularly familiar with the life of the peasants. Reymont, the novelist of the peasants who had also dealt with some problems of emigration in his earlier story, "Righteously," appeared predestined to write such a novel.

He was fully aware of the social significance of emigration.

137

Living in the countryside, he had witnessed many departures and knew how the peasants from the very outset were exposed to cheating and exploitation by various enterprising dealers who arranged for their transportation; this was because the emigrants from the Polish territories occupied by Prussia and Austria, the latter particularly disposed toward emigration on a mass scale, lacked any form of official protection. He also knew of cases of physical persecution by the Russian authorities violently opposed to releasing the political subjects of the Empire.

Zdzislaw Debicki, who later accompanied Reymont to the United States, noted how deeply the novelist was concerned with the question of emigration and literature:

He had been dreaming for a long time about such a novel as a necessary supplement to *The Peasants*, since he thought there could not be a full presentation of the nation without considering emigration, and since emigration played such an important role, to neglect it in Polish literature was a culpable matter.[1]

It was years before Reymont could cross the Atlantic to gather the first-hand material which, unfortunately, never was fictionalized. Since his youth he had dreamt about a trip to the United States, and during his early contacts with the spiritualists he had considered undertaking one. Later, when he settled down in France, his writing prevented him from extensive traveling. The outbreak of World War I made it practically impossible; he spent those years in Poland.

When Poland regained independence in 1918, the authorities began to think seriously about establishing a close official relationship between the reborn country and the millions of Polish immigrants to the United States, who were known as "Polonia." This idea was first suggested by the Polish National Committee established in Paris in 1917 and closely related to the efforts of the Polish Central Relief Committee of America and Comité Général de Suisse pour les Victimes de la Guerre en Pologne created during the war by two leaders in Polish intellectual and artistic life, the world-renowned virtuoso, Ignacy Paderewski and the Nobel Prize winner in literature Henryk Sienkiewicz. After its official recognition by the United States, the Committee

began to search for someone who was well known to represent
Poland effectively to Polonia. Reymont seemed to be a natural
choice because of his prestige in the peasant movement and his
literary endeavors.

As soon as regular diplomatic relations between the United
States and Poland were established, the first official Polish
delegation set out for America. On June 2, 1919 the first Polish
consul general, Konstanty Buszczynski, came aboard the S.S.
"Canada" with a group of representatives. Reymont was unoffi-
cially attached to the delegation whose real mission was to
establish cultural ties between the old country and American
Polonia. During his brief visit to the United States, Reymont
traveled widely in the Polish communities of Chicago, Pittsburgh, Buffalo, Cleveland, and many other cities, gathering
materials and making notes for a novel about the problems of
emigration and immigrants. An American writer, Rupert Hughes,
who met Reymont shortly after his arrival, wrote in The New
York *Times*:

He comes to America in search of materials not laurels, and has
already disappeared among the Polish peasants, who have been
his chief sbuject. There are millions of them in America on farms,
in factories, and in mines, and he intends to study them in their
new environment in order to portray them with that fidelity which
has won him profound respect in Europe.[2]

In the summer of 1919 during his stay in the United States
Reymont met Franck Louis Schoell, who was teaching French
literature at the University of Chicago.[3] Schoell had just completed the translation of the first two volumes of *The Peasants*.
Reymont read and approved the French translation, and in
Chicago signed the contract for its publication in France which,
incidentally, did not take place until 1925, after Reymont received the Nobel Prize. He also signed a contract with Putnam
for publication of the English translation of the novel, which
eventually appeared in 1924-25.

These business matters did not keep him from meeting the
Polish immigrants, telling them about the new Poland and
recalling war experiences. An account of Reymont's public

lecture on September 7, 1919, held in a local theater, was published in a Polish newspaper, *Sokol Polski* (Polish Falcon), in
Pittsburgh. In "a series of recollections," as the novelist called
it, he described vividly the occupation during World War I,
stressing in particular the German terror and atrocities and the
Polish spirit of patriotic resistance. Volunteers from the Polish
army organized in the United States, who had fought against
Germany were in the audience, and Reymont recognized the
importance of their patriotic action along with the work done
by the many Polish organizations in America for Polish war
relief. He concluded his speech with words which must have had
an electrifying effect on his listeners who had left the old country
during the years of partitions: "Raise your heads! Poland is
free! The chains have fallen! You are the sons of the free
sovereign Polish Republic!"[4]

When Reymont left for Poland in September 1919 he could
have considered his official mission accomplished. The contacts
had been established, promises of further cooperation made, and
the road for even closer cultural and economic relations opened.
But the other assignment he had undertaken before crossing the
ocean still seemed far away. Although Hughes, who served as
Reymont's host in the United States, was told that the novelist
"is now working on a cycle consisting of six novels, one of which
will have America as a background," the tremendous stress of
the trip, lectures, and meetings must have so exhausted Reymont
that he was not able to write at all.

Soon after his return to Poland he was asked to take part
in another mission to the United States, this one economic.
Emerging from the postwar chaos, Poland was deeply shaken
by a depression, and only substantial foreign aid could save
the country from complete economic disaster. The sale of
dollar war-bonds among Poles residing in America was decided
upon. A new delegation headed by Franciszek Stefczyk, the
well-known founder of cooperative loan institutions for farmers, included Reymont and his friend, the literary critic, Debicki.
Despite his poor health, Reymont was full of energy and hope,
and aboard the S.S. "New York" he kept meticulous notes and
spent long hours working on his "American novel." In New

York he continued writing in his hotel room until late at night, and he kept to that routine on his trips to Washington, D.C., Philadelphia, Baltimore, and Chicago. But he did not feel at ease in America. Accustomed to the literary cafés of Paris and Poland, he missed the opportunity to meet people and relax, to discuss literature and to engage in friendly gossip. A Polish restaurant in Chicago was a poor substitute for a Parisian literary café. Once, supposedly, he exclaimed in despair: "What a vile country, where there is no place to sit down and to chat a little."[5] New York City he found repulsive with its "materialism and commercialism," and he declared that eventually it would "turn to ashes, for there are not ten just men here."[6] The anti-urban attitude expressed in his novels and stories came to a head during that hot summer of 1920 in the giant city.

He tried to escape the city as often as possible and spent several leisurely week-ends at Hughes's estate in Bedford Hills, New York. More often he visited Polish farmers and miners in Pennsylvania. Even in Chicago he preferred the Polish settlements along Milwaukee Avenue to his elegant hotel on Michigan Boulevard. And always, avoiding publicity and keeping silent during official meetings, he kept searching for materials for a sequel to *The Peasants*, dealing with the fates of his characters on the other side of the ocean. Four years later, shortly before he died, he told Jan Sliwowski in an interview:

Now I am starting a large novel in six parts, under the general title *From the Peasants' Nest*. It will be somehow a continuation of *The Peasants*, with the future fates of some of them and their families. Mateusz goes to America and successfully works "in the foreign land," which will be the title of my first novel to come. The seminarian becomes an enlightened priest and an activist. The others become more prominent in vocational professions, or through marriage, associate themselves with the manor in order to achieve a common welfare.[7]

Apparently the cycle of the novels was well established in the author's mind during his second visit to the United States. Unfortunately he did not live long enough to write it. The course of history even prevented him from gathering all the material. In the summer of 1920 the Soviet invasion of Poland became an immediate danger as Budenny's armies rolled through the eastern provinces toward Warsaw. The very existence of the newly reborn country was at stake, and the desperate situation caused Polish patriots grave concern. As an ardent patriot and as a writer who must witness with his own eyes history in the making, Reymont felt an urge to be in his country in this time of mortal danger. He changed his plans and left for Warsaw by way of Paris, but a new attack of illness prevented him from arriving in time to see the brilliant Polish victory in August 1920, known as "the miracle at the Vistula." His stay in the United States had been interrupted without considerable literary results. What the novelist brought back was, in fact, of very little literary value.

His American trips provided Reymont with topics for a novelette, *The Princess,* and two short stories, "The Return" and "A Confession." In spite of their insignificance compared to his novels and other stories, they deserve critical attention both as sketches for the planned novel and as vignettes from the life of Polonia.

The longest, *The Princess*, can only be regarded as a mistake. It is the melodramatic story of a group of Polish revolutionary socialists working in Chicago for German money, who try to disrupt the Socialist movement from within. Even the title of the novelette indicates Reymont's general ideological confusion. An allegedly aristocratic girl is fighting for Socialism under the pseudonym "The Princess"; her accomplice and boss, a Count with the improbable name Toporczyk Wyhowski, proves to be "a traitor, a gangster, and a spy" all at once, and his past includes cheating, stealing, and various other sins. A counterbalance to that pair of "Polish aristocrats," a noble American with the unimaginative name of Jack Brown, "a Quaker and aristocrat" from Boston, is motivated by love for "the princess" and finally joins the Polish legion and goes to war for Poland's independence!

The plot concerns the ideological transformation of "the princess." She goes through a series of bitter disappointments: first when "Topor" reveals himself as totally evil, then when she discovers their subversive actions are morally wrong, and finally when she comprehends how deeply she is loved by the superhumanly idealistic Jack. Realizing what she has done, she breaks off with the Socialists to start a new life and to repair whatever can be repaired.

This improbable story is set against the realistic background of Polish settlements in Chicago during World War I. Some scenes, especially those showing the genuine enthusiasm of the Polish volunteers who join the American army, are in the best tradition of Reymont's historical fiction. The cheering crowds, the dialogues, and the scenery disclose the sure hand of a master, but those few pages disappear into the general confusion of ideas and facts which make the story artistically grotesque. Reymont's incompatibility with American life and its realities adds to the confusion. He had more than a sufficient background to deal with the peasants in Poland, but he could not grasp either the meaning or the idiom of an entirely new setting.

For example, in *The Princess* and the two remaining stories he used a peculiar language which was supposed to be Polish-American slang, a combination of badly mutilated English words twisted into Polish constructions. There is adequate evidence that such forms exist, as H. L. Mencken demonstrates, for example, in his study, *The American Language*,[8] but Reymont's familiarity with English was too superficial to enable him to recreate them in his stories. His characters say "good-bye" instead of "good morning," address each other using Christian names following "Mister," and so on. In several cases double meanings make the language hardly comprehensible to the reader: in "The Return" the word *rekordy* (records) is used to mean phonographic records, while in Polish it could mean only records in sport. It is doubtful whether the story could ever be understood by readers in Poland. On the other hand, Reymont did reproduce faithfully the broken Polish of young people who use many English words in Polish sentences in just the way that Mencken recorded them. For instance, a character in "The Return" declares:

Cip gaj! Chcialby tylko kisowac. Nading doing, oblizuj sie smakiem. Trafil mi sie fajn kawaler, ma swoją kotedź.

(A cheap guy. He'd like only to kiss. Nothing doing, he won't taste it. I've got a fine fellow, he has his cottage.)[9]

"The Return," a vignette written in December, 1920, half a year after Reymont went back to Poland, illustrates some of the problems Reymont must have heard about from the Polish miners in Pennsylvania. The protagonist of his story, Michal, has spent eighteen years working in the mines for just one purpose: to go back to the old country with sufficient money to buy a piece of land. Saving from his more than modest wages, he finally buys by proxy a former mansion close to his native village, and as the story opens he is getting ready for the trip, which is strongly opposed by his family and the Polish priest in the mining town. The priest is mostly concerned about his parish, which will be taken over by Irishmen if the Polish miners leave. Michal's father-in-law tries to make him aware of the insurmountable social differences he will encounter in the old country run by "magnates, fat excellencies, the pretensions of the gentry, with their extravagances." A tragic accident at the mine finally prevents Michal from fulfilling his dream: as he lies dying he only regrets that he will never go back to the country of his birth.

The story is well composed, dramatic, and apparently based on facts from the life of a Polish community, but it does not touch upon any major issues. Playing on emotions, it emphasizes a particular case rather than generalizes problems of the immigrants, and has little importance as either a social document or as an artistic achievement.

More valuable in both respects is "A Confession," a story written almost two years later, after Reymont had time to gain perspective and think over his impressions of both trips. Subtitle "From the Life of American Polonia," the story deals with the ruthless methods of the Irish clergy, who are determined to take over the primacy in the Roman Catholic church in the United States. Against the well-sustained, tense atmosphere of a gathering storm, a dying man stubbornly refuses to confess to the Irish priest, his "enemy with whom there is no common language." Convinced by his daughter, who translates and also tries to bridge the gap between the Pole and the priest, he argues that he will not go to the church since the Irish "have stolen it from the Poles, driven out our pastor, chased away our nuns, and now are making our children Irish." He prefers to confess his great sin in front of a picture of the holy Madonna; he had murdered his wife.

"A Confession" is highly dramatic. Compact, well composed, and artistically flawless, it resembles the best stories of Reymont's early period. It exceeds both of those discussed above in realism and the weight of the moral problem. All of the American stories, however, remained rather sketchy, and did not contribute to the world fame the author was about to enjoy shortly after his return to Poland. For, without Reymont's knowledge a silent battle was being waged for the world's highest literary honor, the Nobel Prize.

CHAPTER 11

The Nobel Prize

W HEN Henryk Sienkiewicz was awarded the Nobel Prize in literature in 1905, he addressed the Swedish Academy in Stockholm on the significance of his award to Poland:

Those who have the right to compete for the prize established by the noble philanthropist do not belong to the people of one tribe, and do not inhabit one country. All nations of the world compete for that prize, represented by their poets and writers. Therefore, the distinguished areopagus which awards that prize, and the dignified monarch who hands it out, crown not a poet alone but simultaneously the nation whose son that poet is. . . . Although the distinction is precious to all, how much more precious it must be for a son of Poland! . . . She had been considered dead, and here is one of the thousand proofs that she is alive. She had been considered unable to think and work, and here is the proof that she is active. . . . She had been considered conquered, and here is a new proof that she knows how to win.[1]

The award was presented for his novel *Quo Vadis?*, which won Sienkiewicz international acclaim because of numerous translations in English, German, and French all of which appeared in 1896, the year of publication in Polish.

The Peasants had to wait much longer for foreign recognition. In 1912 Jan Kaczkowski translated it into German, and for the next ten years that translation was the single Western European version available. Reymont remained unknown to non-Polish critics and readers. In spite of an article by the distinguished French-Polish critic, Théodore de Wyzewa, published in *Revue des deux mondes*[2] in 1910, there was general silence about Reymont until 1918, when Franck Louis Schoell wrote enthusiastically about him in *Revue de Paris* and attracted the attention of the French publisher C. Payot to *The Peasants*.

Even then, the international fame of the novel, which had been recognized in Poland as a modern classic, was acquired very slowly. The Polish Academy of Arts and Sciences (P. A. U.) recommended Reymont for the Nobel Prize as soon as Poland emerged from the chaos of war; three years later, in a new attempt to win a place for Poland in world literature, the same institution proposed Zeromski, beginning a controversy about the choice between the two writers which lasted for the next fifty years. The Academy's sudden change reflected that unwilling competition which seemed to bind the two authors together throughout their lives, until in 1925 they died a few days apart.[3]

Indeed, after the great authors of Realistic fiction had died or had ceased writing at the beginning of the twentieth century, these two novelists represented the best in Polish fiction for a quarter of a century. Zeromski and Reymont, born in 1864 and 1867 respectively, totally different in their philosophies, ways of life, literary interests, and artistic methods, seemed to compete all that time for the primacy in Polish fiction. Their work, which began to appear in the 1890's eventually attracted the attention not only of Polish critics but also of the Nobel Prize committee. Apparently, only the personal opinion of its President, Archbishop Natan Söderblom tipped the scale, when he pronounced Zeromski an author with whom he "would not like to acquaint the Swedish reader."[4] The preference of one writer over another divided critics equally both in Poland and in the committee. In his country Zeromski was generally considered more important than Reymont intellectually and artistically, but some critics strongly opposed his candidacy because of his social radicalism, political opinions, and, in some cases, moral offensiveness. Reymont did not offend in these ways. This was one of the reasons why Reymont was supported by the Swedish critic, Fredrik Böök, an official consultant to the Nobel Prize committee who, as early as 1918, had compared *The Peasants* with Homer's *Iliad,* emphasizing the epic values of the novel.[5] Böök, editor of the powerful *Svenska Dagbladet,* was generally regarded as a spokesman for public opinion, while his opponent, Alfred Jansen, who advised the committee on Slavic

literature and favored Zeromski, represented primarily his own
views. When Jansen died in 1921, even the weighty voice of Ad.
Stender-Petersen could not turn the committee against Böök's
opinion. In 1924 Stender-Petersen wrote:

Zeromski is the restless intellectual, full of clashing contradictions,
submerged in egocentric searchings and aflame with unanswerable
questions and insoluble doubts. Reymont is the calm, harmonious
poet, filled with the consciousness of life's unity and meaning, and
holding the center of existence in his own soul. Never has Zeromski
succeeded in equaling Reymont's ability to produce masterpieces
of faultless composition and to meet life with undisturbed, poetic
calm; but he has, on the other hand, always excelled Reymont in
depth of feeling, in artistic variety, in refinement of language and
temperament.[6]

Political issues disclosed only years later were as much involved
in the choice as critical issues. Lorentowicz considers the support of the Peasant Party, at that time influential in the Polish
government, to have been a strong force in favor of Reymont's
candidacy.[7] This opinion has been challenged by Alfred Wysocki, a former Polish envoy to Stockholm who as recently as
1955 inquired about that matter at the Swedish Academy and
received a negative answer.[8] At any rate, the whole affair finally
was removed from the hands of the Polish opponents to Reymont and was decisively settled by the Swedish committee
itself, although not without some difference of opinion.

Although, according to the official citation, the Academy
awarded Reymont the prize for *The Peasants,* according to
Svenska Dagbladet of November 14, 1924, the prize also expressed "the sympathy of the Swedish people for the spiritual
culture of that highly gifted Polish nation in the moment of the
triumph of a resurrected Poland." The Swedish press resounded
with similar opinions in a great majority of the articles devoted
to Reymont, articles which number more than 120 immediately
following the award.

This highest literary honor came too late. The ailing author
was not able to attend the ceremonies in Stockholm and sent
instead a brief autobiography.[9] In a private letter he wrote to
his friend, Wysocki:

That is terrible! Nobel Prize, money, world-wide fame, and a man who cannot undress without getting very tired. This is a real irony of life, sneering and satanic indeed. Or maybe something else. I do not know whether you know it, but I am deeply religious, and so I accept what befalls me as a disposition of Providence.[10]

Seriously ill, Reymont went to Nice in hope of recovery. The golden medal and the diploma of the Nobel Prize reached him there, as the publicity began to spread widely in Europe and across the ocean. His new fame did not prevent the French customs from charging Reymont 1,000 francs for the medal, and it took the official intervention of the Polish consulate to lift the duty. The critics, however, were more kind than the bureaucrats. Despite some surprise on the part of those who obviously did not want to admit that serious literature existed beyond the boundaries of Western Europe, the majority of critics approved the choice of the Swedish Academy. The fact that Reymont won against such candidates as Grazzia Deledda, Vicente Blasco-Ibáñez, Thomas Hardy, Thomas Mann, Sigrid Undset, and Maxim Gorky impressed even the most skeptical defenders of the supremacy of Western European literatures.

Among the most enthusiastic admirers of Reymont from the time of his first encounter with Polish literature was Schoell, the French translator of *The Peasants*. Although he modestly denies his contribution to Reymont's fame, he must have been instrumental in introducing the Polish novelist's work to literary circles in France as well as the United States, where he had been teaching. In America, Rupert Hughes and Albert Morawski-Nawench, a lecturer at Columbia University, also helped to make Reymont's work known and a Polish scholar, Roman Dyboski, popularized Reymont in the English-speaking world through a series of lectures and articles. The task was not easy. Reymont's supporters had to overcome misunderstanding, prejudice, and even open dislike which resulted, for example, in a curious anonymous review of *The Peasants* in *Time* magazine entitled "Cows, Vodka, Acres, Potatoes, Soil, Love, Hate,"[11] or an editorial in *The New York Times* ironically calling on "the Switzerlands, the Irelands, and the Bengals . . . to run their course in the tourney lists of genius."[12] However, when *The Peasants* was published in English, those opinions were undercut by the popularity of *The Peasants* with the majority of critics and the reading public. It and the other works that followed won Reymont a distinguished place among American readers in the 1920's.[13]

Reymont followed the critical battle closely. In his letter to Schoell he reported with pleasure the publication of the French, English, and Japanese translations, and the external appearance of the books. But he was too ill to continue writing. His correspondence with Schoell ends dramatically, as if peacefully closing for good the controversy over the Nobel Prize.

Today Zeromski died, which is a heavy blow for me for many reasons. He died of a heart attack. He was a couple of years older than I am, but he had a tremendous will for life and energy. It is an irreplaceable loss to Polish literature. I admired him as a writer of genius. Naturally, that sudden death had a bad impact on my own health too. For it is my turn to die now.—

I will not write more.[14]

This letter dated November 20, 1925, was received by Schoell in Berkeley, California, several days after the press had brought him the news that Reymont had died on December 5, 1925.

CHAPTER 12

A Centennial Appraisal

IN 1967 Poland celebrated Reymont's centennial as if to bestow upon the author of *The Peasants* the prominence he had been denied for years. The revival of interest in Reymont's work and biography is indicated by the appearance of more than fifty articles and books on Reymont in 1966 and 1967 alone. Special events celebrated Reymont's birthday on May 7, 1967. At the University of Lodz, the Polish Academy of Sciences organized a special session entitled "Reymont in Literature."[1] In Warsaw, Lodz, Zakopane, and several other places connected with the author, commemorative plaques and statues were unveiled. The Post Office issued a special postage stamp. The publishing house "Wydawnictwo Lodzkie" in Lodz announced the forthcoming publication of the complete edition of his works, while several young scholars began to work on an edition of his letters and other material hitherto either unknown or unpublished. Many other countries all over Europe and America held similar celebrations and announced new editions of his novels and stories. Reymont's work and his personal writings began to emerge from forty years of oblivion.

The comments of two critics, expressed during the centennial, suggested that Reymont was still due a share of critical attention. A Polish critic, Tadeusz Drewnowski, ended his essay with this appeal to public opinion:

We are in certain debt to Reymont. Rather than with a fête we should celebrate his centennial by dusting off and publishing a new selection of his works. The work of the greatest self-made talent in Poland needs its new canon. Today we can see a new classic of the turn of the century emerging from an anticlassical period. An original classic, too, such as we have never had. To be read.[2]

151

Professor Jan Zygmunt Jakubowski, the leading Polish specialist in Modernist literature, wrote similiarly in an article entitled "On Reymont, Most Personally." After admittting his own preference for several other novelists of that period, he concluded:

But Reymont still awaits his biographer. . . . Reymont's literary biography has to be written, too, a story of the intellectual development of an autodidact who in the twenty-sixth year of his life left a modest position at a small railroad station to take in a short time a high position on the Polish Parnassus, and to crown his unusual life with the highest literary prize in the world. Above all, the work of Reymont, so complex and uneven in its artistic form and ideological content, calls for new research.[3]

Recent Polish criticism still calls for new research on Reymont and his work. In print today are the first volumes of a critical edition of Reymont's first novels, painstakingly prepared by Zygmunt Szweykowski, which will probably take years to complete.[4] A bibliography of criticism in languages other than Polish is badly needed to determine Reymont's impact on world literature and to establish its scope. Even so, one can appraise Reymont's influence on the basis of materials now available.

Even though his work has not been given adequate attention in his native country, Reymont remains one of the most popular Polish authors abroad. In the decade from 1957 to 1966 alone, *The Peasants* was published in Belgium, Czechoslovakia, Denmark, Germany, Holland, Hungary, Spain, Switzerland, and Yugoslavia, while his other novels and short stories and excerpts from them appeared in seventeen countries, including China.[5] This is a record which, we may safely assume, only a few of Reymont's competitors for the Nobel Prize in 1924 can match forty years later. The lasting interest in his work indicates that it contains values reaching far beyond national boundaries. His major novels can be read with the same interest today as half a century ago. They neither fade nor appear old-fashioned, but arouse the same emotions and appeal to the reader with the same intensity as they did to previous generations. A distinguished Polish critic, Waclaw Borowy, stated thirty years ago commenting on the structure of Reymont's work,

... the greatness of which lies in its simplicity. The life of a peasant is dependent on the change of seasons. Every season has its peculiarities which recur periodically every year. A year forms a close whole in this respect. . . . In this plan the order of life itself imposed the line of construction. Without any particular intellectual effort the structure grew naturally and strongly. It is logical as well as it is elemental. This is also its basic originality.[6]

"It is logical as well as it is elemental" is the basic formula for understanding Reymont's lasting importance. No matter whether we read his novels and short stories as realistic documents of the epoch or as symbols of the everlasting struggle of the human spirit, whether we apply to them the simple method of Naturalistic "life-likeness," or search in them for archetypes, the formula is valid, at least for those works which retain their artistic value. Although those works of Reymont's which were written in accordance with passing trends must slip quietly into oblivion, the bulk of his work remains alive. His theatrical and social novels in some respects can stand comparison with the indisputable mastery of *The Peasants*. His historical trilogy is at least as good as any major historical novel of its time, and a great many of his short stories can withstand the criteria of changing artistic taste and more sophisticated criticism. They contain logical and elemental truths, both human and artistic. Reymont's work does not age but speaks to us with the same strong, human voice as it spoke to many generations, in many languages, in many countries throughout the world.

Notes and References

Chapter One

1. Manfred Kridl, *A Survey of Polish Literature and Culture* ('s Gravenhage, 1956), iii.
2. Kridl, *op. cit.*, 476.

Chapter Two

1. Zdzislaw Debicki, *Wladyslaw Stanislaw Reymont—laureat Nobla* (W. S. Reymont, the Nobel Prize Winner) (Warsaw, 1925), 34.
2. Adam Grzymala-Siedlecki, *Niepospolici ludzie w dniu swoim powszednim* (Unusual People in Their Every-day Lives) (Cracow, 1961), 254-55.
3. Reprinted in Julian Krzyzanowski, *Wladyslaw Stanislaw Reymont. Tworca i dzielo* (W. S. Reymont. The Writer and his Work) (Lwow, 1937), 2-8.
4. A letter to Tadeusz Mikulski, reprinted in his *Spotkania wroclawskie* (Wroclaw Encounters) (Wroclaw, 1950), 342.
5. An original French version in Reymont's manuscripts collection in Zaklad Narodowy im. Ossolinskich, Wroclaw, No. 6977/1.
6. "Wladyslaw Stanislaw Reymont. Lato 1894 za granica" (W. S. Reymont. Summer 1894 Abroad), *Zeszyty Wroclawskie* (Wroclaw Notebooks), II, 1 (1948), 27.
7. Ms. in Zaklad Narodowy im. Ossolinskich, No. 6954/7. The entries from Reymont's diary quoted subsequently come from the same source.
8. "Nad uczczonym grobem" (Over the venerable grave), *Tygodnik Illustrowany* (Illustrated Weekly), 1926, 2, 24.
9. "W. S. Reymont. Lato 1894 ..." (Summer 1894 Abroad ...), 19.
10. Jan Lorentowicz, *Spojrzenie wstecz* (Looking Back) (Cracow, 1957).

Chapter Three

1. René Wellek and Austin Warren, *Theory of Literature* (New York, 1956), 205.

2. See Julian Krzyzanowski, *Romans polski wieku XVI* (Polish 16th Century Romance) (Lublin, 1934), 5-7; Michal Glowinski, Aleksandra Okopien, Janusz Slawinski, *Zarys teorii literatury* (An Outline of Theory of Literature) (Warsaw, 1967), 367 ff.

3. Ignacy Matuszewski, *O tworczosci i tworcach* (On Creativity and the Authors) (Warsaw, 1965), 211-12.

4. Ostap Ortwin, "O teatrze tragicznym" (On Tragic Theater) in Jan Zygmunt Jakubowski (ed.), *Polska krytyka literacka (1800-1918)* (Polish Literary Criticism [1800-1918]) (Warsaw, 1959), IV, 299.

5. The term Positivism is generally used in history of Polish literature with reference to the period between 1863 and 1890, denoting an ideological trend based on scientific principles and a sober, positive attitude toward political and economic problems. In literature it coincided with the realistic method in fiction, and with the growth of the novel and short story as genres.

6. In *Literatura polska w okresie realizmu i naturalizmu* (Polish Literature in the Periods of Realism and Naturalism) (Warsaw, 1965), I, 14-15.

7. Adam Grzymala-Siedlecki, *op. cit.*, 249.

8. Some similarities between Dostoevsky and Reymont have been mentioned in passing by J. Krzyzanowski in his study on Reymont, *op. cit.*, 36, 41.

9. Jan Lorentowicz, "Nasi mlodzi" (Our Young Ones), *Przeglad Tygodniowy* (Weekly Review), 1898, 15.

10. *The Ferments* (Warsaw, 1962), 340. All translations of Reymont's works quoted from the Polish originals are by the present writer.

11. Lorentowicz, *op. cit.*, 18.

12. Lech Budrecki, *Wladyslaw Reymont* (Warsaw, 1953), 55.

13. *Ibid.*, 69.

14. Krzyzanowski, *op. cit.*, 44.

15. The Ms. in Zaklad Narodowy im. Ossolinskich, Wroclaw, No. 6960. For the minor differences between the two versions see the editor's note in Adam Bar's edition of Reymont's *Pisma* (Works) (Warsaw, 1950), V, 464-66.

16. Donald W. Heiney, *Essentials of Contemporary Literature* (Great Neck, N. Y., 1954), 34.

Chapter Four

1. Quoted in the critical edition of *Ziemia obiecana* (The Promised Land), Zygmunt Szweykowski, ed. (Warsaw, 1965), 702.

2. Jan Lorentowicz, *Mloda Polska* (Young Poland) (Warsaw, 1909), II, 162.

3. *Ziemia obiecana* (The Promised Land), 21.

4. *Ibid.*, 153-54.

5. As Lorentowicz sarcastically remarks: "Finalement il devient tolstoïste." *Ladislas Reymont* (Warsaw, 1925), 16.

6. *Ziemia obiecana* (The Promised Land), 699.

7. *Ibid.*, 361.

8. Krzyzanowski, *op. cit.*, 201-4, compares the story of the Jaskolskis with similar motifs in Maria Konopnicka's short stories and poetry.

9. *Ibid.*, 191.

10. Adam Grzymala-Siedlecki in the editor's introduction to Reymont's *Pisma* (Works) (Warsaw, 1924), V, 17.

11. Alfred Wysocki, *Sprzed pol wieku* (From Half a Century Ago) (Cracow, 1956), 155.

12. Antoni Potocki, *Szkice i wrazenia literackie* (Literary Sketches and Impressions) (Lwow, 1903), 50.

13. *Ziemia obiecana* (The Promised Land), 7.

14. Maria Rzeuska, *"Chlopi" Reymonta* (Reymont's "Peasants") (Warsaw, 1950), 114-15.

15. *Ziemia obiecana* (The Promised Land), 350.

16. *Ibid.*, 430.

17. Julian Krzyzanowski, *Neoromantyzm polski 1890-1918* (Polish Neo-Romanticism 1890-1918) (Wroclaw, 1963), 253.

18. *Dziela wybrane* (Selected Works) (Cracow, n.d.), II, 224.

Chapter Five

1. Budrecki, *op. cit.*, 23.

2. Krzyzanowski, *op. cit.*, 76.

3. Matuszewski, *op. cit.*, 230.

4. *Ibid.*, 229.

5. *Dziela wybrane* (Selected Works), II, 121.

6. *Ibid.*, II, 125.

7. For a discussion of that form of speech in fiction see Kazimierz Woycicki, "Z pogranicza stylistyki" (From the Borderland of Studies in Style), *Przeglad Humanistyczny* (Humanist Review), 1922, I, 75-100; Glowinski, *op. cit.*, 354-55.

8. *Dziela wybrane* (Selected Works) (Cracow, n.d.), II, 184.

9. *Ibid.*, II, 182-83.

Chapter Six

1. Krzyzanowski, *Neoromantyzm polski* (Polish Neo-Romanticism), 17.

2. Matuszewski, *op. cit.*, 239.

3. Wysocki, "Trzy spotkania z Reymontem" (Three Meetings with Reymont), *Tworczosc* (Creativity), 1947, III, 7/8, 43.

4. Wysocki, *Sprzed pol wieku* (From Half a Century Ago), 156.

5. Rzeuska, *op. cit.*, 3. The Ms. of *The Peasants* is in Zaklad Narodowy im. Ossolinskich, Wroclaw.

6. Lorentowicz, *Spojrzenie wstecz* (Looking Back), 9 ff.

7. Wysocki, *op. cit.*, 153.

8. Grzymala-Siedlecki, *Niepospolici ludzie . . .* (Unusual People . . .), 264-65.

9. Dmitrij Cizevskij, *Das Heilige Russland. Russische Geistesgeschichte 10-17 Jahrhundert* (Hamburg, 1959), 21.

10. Budrecki, *op. cit.*, 118-20.

11. Rzeuska, *op. cit.*, 25.

12. Krzyzanowski, *Reymont . . .* , 112-30.

13. Rzeuska, *op. cit.*, 18.

14. Jan Nepomucen Miller, *Zaraza w Grenadzie* (A Pest in Granada) (Warsaw, 1926), 120-26.

15. *Chlopi* (The Peasants), Warsaw, 1965, IV, 294.

16. See Julije Benesic, "Selo Lipce" (The Village of Lipce), *Hrvatska Revija* (Croatian Review), VI (1933), 1, 28-36; Monika Warnenska, *Sladami pisarzy* (In the Footsteps of the Writers) (Warsaw, 1964), 304-30; Barbara Wachowicz, "Powrot do Lipiec" (A Return to Lipce), *Kultura* (Culture) (Warsaw), 1967, 23.

17. Rzeuska, *op. cit.*, 42.

18. Franck Louis Schoell, "Étude sur le roman paysan naturaliste. D'Émile Zola à Ladislas Reymont," *Revue de la littérature comparée*, VII (1927), 254-99.

19. See Ignacy Fik, *Rodowod spoleczny literatury polskiej* (The Social Genealogy of Polish Literature) (Cracow, 1946); for a detailed account of the critical opinions on *The Peasants* particularly in the 1920's and 1930's see Tine Debeljak, *Reymontovi Kmetje v luci knjizevne kritike* (Reymont's Peasants in Best Critical Studies) (Ljubljana, 1936).

20. Franck Louis Schoell, *Les Paysans polonais vus par un des leurs* (Paris, 1918).

21. Among the studies devoted to these issues and the relationship between Russian and Anglo-Saxon literature, particularly the problems

of realism in the "new school of fiction," see Dorothy Brewster, *East-West Passage* (London, 1954), 150-55.

22. William Dean Howells, *My Literary Passions* (New York, 1895). Reprinted in W. D. Howells, *European and American Masters* (New York, 1963), 41 ff.

23. Stefania Skwarczynska, *Wstep do nauki o literaturze* (An Introduction to the Study of Literature) (Warsaw, 1954), I, 325.

24. Rupert Hughes, "Ladislas Reymont—Nobel Prize Winner," *Poland,* 1925, 6.

Chapter Seven

1. Eliza Orzeszkowa, *Listy* (Letters) (Warsaw, 1937), I, 361.

2. Wilhelm Feldman, *Wspolczesna literatura polska* (Contemporary Polish Literature) (Cracow, 1930), 466.

3. Henryk Markiewicz, *Prus i Zeromski* (Prus and Zeromski) (Warsaw, 1964), 301.

4. Ms. of Reymont's notes in Zaklad Narodowy im. Ossolinskich, Wroclaw, No. 6973/1.

5. Reymont, *Pisma* (Works), A. Bar, ed. (Warsaw, 1949), XIX, 405-11.

6. Adam Szelagowski, "Artyzm historyczny Reymonta" (Reymont's Historical Artistry), *Tygodnik Illustrowany* (Illustrated Weekly), 1926, 2, 26.

7. Krzyzanowski, *Reymont . . . ,* 134-37, Budrecki, *op. cit.,* 185. See also Henryk Markiewicz, "Poslowie" (Afterword) to Reymont, *Dziela wybrane* (Selected Works) (Cracow, n.d.), XII, 354.

8. *Dziela wybrane* (Selected Works), X, 36-37.

9. *Ibid.,* X, 185.

10. Oscar Halecki, *A History of Poland* (Chicago, 1966), 206-7.

11. *Ibid.,* 206.

12. This fragment is usually printed as an addendum to the novel.

13. *Dziela wybrane* (Selected Works), XII, 17-18.

14. *Ibid.,* XII, 22.

Chapter Eight

1. D. S. Mirsky, *A History of Russian Literature* (New York, 1958), 388-89.

2. Thomas Winner, *Chekhov and His Prose* (New York, 1966), 40.

3. *Dziela wybrane* (Selected Works), III, 210.

4. *Dostoevsky,* René Wellek, ed. (Englewood Cliffs, N. J., 1962), 116. In a brief study on Polish and Russian fiction "Le Roman polonais

du XIXᵉ siècle et la création romanesque européene" (in *Literatura, Komparatystyka, Folklor*, Warsaw, 1968, pp. 495-515), Janina Kulczyka-Saloni points out well known similarities between *The Peasants* and Zola's *La Terre* as well as certain affinities between *The Promised Land* and Zola's trilogy *Trois Villes* but does not explore Reymont's industrial novel in comparison with Kuprin's *Moloch* (1896) or a close relationship between *The Dreamer* and *Duel*.

5. Krzyzanowski, *Reymont* . . . , 38.

6. Cf. T. Mikulski, "Reymont i duchy" (Reymont and Ghosts) in *Spotkania wroclawskie* (Wroclaw Encounters), 350.

7. Lorentowicz, *Spojrzenie wstecz* (Looking Back), 9 ff.

Chapter Nine

1. Budrecki, *op. cit.*, 143.

2. *Dziela wybrane* (Selected Works), III, 25.

3. Halecki, *op. cit.*, 267.

4. Adolf Nowaczynski, "Ostatnie dzielo Reymonta" (Reymont's Last Work), *Mysl Narodowa* (National Thought), 1925, 11.

5. Krzyzanowski, *op. cit.*, 170.

Chapter Ten

1. Zdzislaw Debicki, "Reymont w Ameryce" (Reymont in America), *Tygodnik Illustrowany* (Illustrated Weekly), 1926, 2, 34.

2. New York *Times*, 1919 (July 13), 3.

3. Bronislaw Miazgowski, ed., *Reymont we Francji* (Reymont in France) (Warsaw, 1967), 49-57. See also Leon Orlowski, ed., *Reymont w Ameryce* (Reymont in America) (Warsaw, 1970).

4. *Sokol Polski* (Polish Falcon), 1919 (September 25), 3. I should like to express my gratitude to Mr. Arthur L. Waldo for making these materials available for this study.

5. Debicki, *Ibid*.

6. *Ibid.*, 38.

7. Quoted in Krzyzanowski, *op. cit.*, 164. A plan of chapters for that novel is in Ms., Zaklad Narodowy im. Ossolinskich, 6977/II.

8. H. L. Mencken, *The American Language* (New York, 1936), 673-75. More recently it was given new attention in Franciszek Lyra, "The Polish Language in the United States," *The Polish Review*, VII, 2, 81-95.

9. In a collection of short stories, *Krosnowa i swiat* (Krosnowa and the World) (Warsaw, 1928), 322. Some notes made by Reymont on Polish-American speech in Ms., Zaklad Narodowy im. Ossolinskich,

6977/II. I am grateful to Dr. B. Wieczorkiewicz for making these notes available for this study.

Chapter Eleven

1. Henryk Sienkiewicz, *Dziela* (Works) (Warsaw, 1951), XL, 140.
2. Théodore de Wyzewa, "Un romancier polonais," *Revue des deux mondes*, 1910 (September 15).
3. See Roman Dyboski, "Zeromski and Reymont," *The Slavonic Review* (1926), IV, 552-61.
4. Wysocki, *Sprzed pol wieku* (From Half a Century Ago), 180.
5. Fredrik Böök, *Essayer och kritiker*, IV (1918).
6. Ad. Stender-Petersen, "Reymont, Winner of the Nobel Prize," *The Living Age*, 1924, 165-66.
7. Lorentowicz, *Spojrzenie wstecz* (Looking Back), 14 ff. See also Stanislaw Wedkiewicz, "Dookola literackiej nagrody Nobla" (Around the Literary Nobel Prize) *Przeglad Wspolczesny* (Contemporary Review) (1925), IV, 41, 335-92.
8. Wysocki, *op. cit.*, 193-94.
9. *Nobel Lectures: Literature, 1901-67* (New York, Horst Frenz, ed., 1969), 218-22.
10. Wysocki, *op. cit.*, 189.
11. *Time*, 1924 (December 1).
12. New York *Times*, 1924 (November 16).
13. For an account on American reception of *The Peasants*, see Jerzy R. Krzyzanowski, "Amerykanskie poglosy 'Chlopow' Reymonta," (American Echoes of Reymont's "Peasants"), *Kongres Wspolczesnej Nauki i Kultury Polskiej na Obczyznie* (Congress of Contemporary Polish Science and Culture Abroad) (London, 1970), Vol. I, 285-89.
14. *Reymont we Francji* (Reymont in France), 44.

Chapter Twelve

1. Published later in *Prace Polonistyczne* (Studies in Polish Literature), 1968, XXIV.
2. Tadeusz Drewnowski, "Arcy-oko" (Super-Eye), *Polityka* (Politics), 1967, 24 (537), (June 17), 7.
3. Jan Zygmunt Jakubowski, "O Reymoncie najbardziej osobiscie" (On Reymont Most Personally), *Kultura* (Culture) (Warsaw), 1967, 19 (May 7), 9.
4. *Komediantka* (The Comedienne) (Warsaw, 1961), *Fermenty*

(Ferments) (Warsaw, 1962), *Ziemia obiecana* (The Promised Land) (Warsaw, 1965), *Chlopi* (The Peasants) (Warsaw, 1970).

5. For a complete list of translations and publications cf. *Rocznik literacki* (Literary Yearbook) (Warsaw, 1955 through 1969). For a full bibliography of English translations see Marion Moore Coleman, *Polish Literature in English Translation* (Cheshire, 1963); Jerzy Maciuszko, *The Polish Short Story in English* (Detroit, 1968). Among the studies in languages other than English there appeared a monographic study in Rumanian, *Reymont* by Velea Stan (Bucharest, 1966).

6. Waclaw Borowy, "Reymont," *The Slavonic Review* (1938), XVI, 446.

Selected Bibliography

PRIMARY SOURCES

I Collected Works

Pisma (Works), Adam Grzymala-Siedlecki, ed., 20 vols., Warsaw, 1921-25 (incomplete).
Pisma (Works), Zdzislaw Debicki, ed., 48 vols., Warsaw, 1930-34.
Pisma (Works), Adam Bar, ed., 20 vols., Warsaw, 1948-53 (incomplete.
Dziela wybrane (Selected Works), H. Markiewicz and J. Skornicki, eds., 12 vols., Cracow, 1955-57.

II English Translations

DZIEWICKI, MICHAEL H. *The Peasants,* 4 vols., New York, A. Knopf, 1924-25.
DZIEWICKI, MICHAEL H. *The Promised Land,* 2 vols., New York, A. Knopf, 1927.
OBECNY, EDMUND. *The Comedienne,* New York, A. Knopf, 1920.

SECONDARY SOURCES

I Critical Studies in Polish

BUDRECKI, LECH. *Wladyslaw Reymont.* Warsaw, Czytelnik, 1953. A Marxist presentation of Reymont's fiction as a reflection of his ideology and political involvement.
KOCOWNA, BARBARA. *Reymont.* Warsaw. Ludowa Spoldzielnia Wydawnicza, 1971. A concise biography based on many hitherto unpublished letters. Original photographs.
KRZYZANOWSKI, JULIAN. *Wladyslaw Stanislaw Reymont. Tworca i dzielo* (W. S. Reymont. The Author and His Work). Lwow. Zaklad Narodowy im. Ossolinskich, 1937. A basic monograph on Reymont's works in relation to the history of Polish literature.
RZEUSKA, MARIA. *"Chlopi" Reymonta* (Reymont's *The Peasants*). Warsaw, Towarzystwo Naukowe Warszawskie. 1950. A mono-

graph on *The Peasants* with main emphasis on its linguistic features.

WYKA, KAZIMIERZ. "Proba nowego odczytania *Chlopow*" (An Attempt at a New Reading of *The Peasants*), *Pamietnik Literacki* (Literary Archive) (1968), LIX, 2, 57-105.

II   Critical Works in English

ALMEDINGEN, EDITH M. "Ladislas Reymont—Peasant and Writer," *The English Review*, XLII (January, 1926), pp. 119-22. A short literary biography.

BOROWY, WACLAW. "Reymont," *The Slavonic Review*, XVI (1938), pp. 439-48. An appraisal of Reymont's work with some valuable critical re-evaluations.

BOYD, ERNEST. "Wladyslaw Reymont," *The Saturday Review of Literature*, I, 18 (November 29, 1924), pp. 317-19. A well-documented critical discussion of Reymont's work, contains bibliographical information.

DYBOSKI, ROMAN. "Zeromski and Reymont," *The Slavonic Review*, IV (1926), pp. 552-61. Classical elements in Reymont's work contrasted with romantic character of Zeromski.

HUGHES, RUPERT. "Poland's Peasant Novelist," *The New York Times Magazine* (July 13, 1919), pp. 10, 25. First general information on Reymont and his novels in the U. S. press.

————. "Ladislas Reymont, Winner of the Nobel Prize," *The Literary Digest International Book Review*, III, 3 (February, 1925), p. 171. Some personal reminiscences on Reymont and on his novels, *The Peasants* in particular.

————. "Ladislas Reymont—Nobel Prize Winner," *Poland* I (1925), pp. 5, 6, 45. Brief remarks on Reymont and his work.

KRZYZANOWSKI, JERZY R. "The Promised Land: A Modern Novel," *Studies in Polish Civilization* (New York, 1971), pp. 250-55. A short critical analysis of Reymont's industrial novel.

MORAWSKI-NAWENCH, ALBERT. "Reymont at Home," *Poland*, VI, 12 (December, 1925), pp. 710-15. Some reminiscences of the author's visit with Reymont in Poland. Illustrations.

SCHOELL, FRANCK LOUIS. "Ladislas Reymont, 1868-1925," *California University Chronicle*, XXVIII (1926), pp. 263-67. A critical appraisal of Reymont's life and work.

————. "How Reymont Wrote His Greatest Novel," *The Literary Digest International Book Review*, IV, 2 (January, 1926), 87-88. A popular presentation of Reymont's work.

STENDER-PETERSEN, ADOLF. "Reymont, Winner of the Nobel Prize," *The Living Age*, vol. 324, No. 4202 (January 19, 1925), pp. 165-69. A well-documented and penetrating discussion of Reymont's place in contemporary literature.

ZIELINSKI, THADDEUS. "The Peasant in Polish Literature" (II), *The Slavonic Review*, II (1923-24), 4, pp. 85-100. *The Peasants* discussed as a vital contribution to the image of peasants in Polish literature.

Index

167